ANDREW DELBANCO

REQUIRED READING

Why Our American Classics Matter Now

The Noonday Press ★ Farrar, Straus and Giroux ★ New York

The Noonday Press
A division of Farrar, Straus and Giroux
19 Union Square West, New York 10003

Copyright © 1997 by Andrew Delbanco
All rights reserved
Distributed in Canada by Douglas & McIntyre Ltd.
Printed in the United States of America
Designed by Jonathan D. Lippincott
First published in 1997 by Farrar, Straus and Giroux
First Noonday paperback edition, 1998

The essays in this book have appeared, in different form, in *The New Republic, The New York Review of Books, Raritan,* and *Salmagundi.* "Was Kate Chopin a Feminist?" was originally published, in different form, as "The Half-Life of Edna Pontellier" in *New Essays on the Awakening,* edited by Wendy Martin. Copyright © 1989 by Andrew Delbanco. Reprinted with the permission of Cambridge University Press.

The Library of Congress has catalogued the hardcover edition as follows:
Delbanco, Andrew, 1952–
    Required reading : why our American classics matter now / Andrew Delbanco.
        p.   cm.
    Includes index.
    ISBN 0-374-23007-2 (alk. paper)
    1. American literature—History and criticism—Theory, etc.
2. National characteristics, American, in literature.   3. Politics and literature—United States.   4. Literature and society—United States.   5. Books and reading—United States.   6. Liberalism in literature.   7. Democracy in literature.   8. Canon (Literature)
I. Title.
PS25.D45   1997   97-11229
810.9'358—dc21

To Thomas and Nicholas Delbanco
brothers and good friends

REQUIRED READING

Contents

Preface

This book is about the idea that individual human beings can break free of the structures of thought into which they are born and that, by reimagining the world, they can change it. I have tried to convey the power of this idea by describing some great American writers (certainly not all those who merit the term "classic") who span roughly a century, from the years preceding the Civil War to the eve of World War II. These writers believed, or wished to believe, in the possibility of transcendence, and they exemplified this idea in the art of prose.

I use the words "idea" and "art" with equal devotion in the hope that these chapters may help close the gap that seems today to divide serious writing about literature into two warring camps. On the one hand, instrumentalist critics (who have lately dominated literary discussion in our universities) are chiefly interested in books for what they reveal about the political dimension of human experience. On the other hand, appreciationists (who feel increasingly beleaguered) celebrate books as sources of aesthetic delight. Since I believe that these two ways of reading can and must converge, I would describe this book, at risk of presumption, in the same way that Lionel Trilling nearly fifty years ago described a book of his own: "These are not political essays, they are essays in literary criticism. But they assume the inevitable intimate, if not always obvious, connection between literature and politics."

The politics implicit in classic American writing are those of liberal democracy—a society of individuals restrained within a structure of mutual responsibility but free to pursue happiness by refusing the designated status of their parents, race, sex, or any other limiting accident of birth. These writers celebrated American democracy, or called it to account for its failures, because they believed that individuals, whether born as servants or masters, should be able to break out of what William James called "the circumpressure of [one's] caste and set" to achieve lives of freedom and fulfillment.

Yet all of them, although born long before our "postmodern" era, were well aware that each time we write, or speak, or think, we use a borrowed voice, and are limited by a culture in which, despite the grandeur of its promise, the happiness of some is often built on the degradation of others. They also knew, with Tocqueville, that "in democratic communities, the imagination is compressed when men consider themselves; it expands indefinitely when they think of the state." They believed in the inviolable rights of the free self; but they knew that without common allegiance to the institutions and symbols through which this veneration for the integrity of each and all is expressed, Americans are condemned to anxiety and soul-killing isolation.

Some of them (Stephen Crane, Kate Chopin, Theodore Dreiser, Edith Wharton) wrote darkly about the unbearable loneliness of life without this indispensable completion of the self, but most of them wrote in a spirit of hope. With few exceptions (notably Henry Adams), they held little nostalgia for the jettisoned past, and celebrated the process by which conventions are perpetually dissolved in the restless, dynamic society of the United States. They were as committed to America as they were certain that America had not yet realized its promise. They did not contend that America was somehow God's chosen nation. But they did believe in democracy as a saving way for human beings to find fulfillment in a world without God.

With the exception of Abraham Lincoln, none of these writers was primarily a political thinker. First and last, they were inspired practitioners of the American language. Although they valued the literary achievements of the past, they were determined to enlarge the expressive range of the language beyond where their predecessors had left it. To read them is to experience anew the pleasure that everyone knows who has ever tried to coax a sentence out of the conventional form in which it wants to settle, and who manages to carry it instead toward a new shape, a new gesture, a new style. Recognizing this when it happens on the page is what reading is all about. To do it oneself is to be a writer. Through this *literary* experience—this refusal to submit to precedent, no matter how honored or honorable—we can partake of the democratic faith in the capacity of all human beings to perform the miracle of creation.

Andrew Delbanco
New York City
October 1996

REQUIRED READING

★ 1 ★

Melville's Sacramental Style

The first critical comment that ever struck me as having a real bearing on what writing is all about was Norman Mailer's remark, in *The Armies of the Night*, that "a good half of writing consists of being sufficiently sensitive to the moment to reach for the next promise which is usually hidden in some word or phrase just a shift to the side of one's conscious intent." This seemed right for the same reason that any statement has the ring of truth when you are an adolescent—because it corresponded to my sense of what occasionally happened in my own experience: I would sometimes get caught up (even in a prescribed assignment) by the sentences themselves and the world would disappear and I would work in a nervous silence out of which a real phrase or two would emerge, as if dictated from someone outside the room.

But the most lasting experience I have had that keeps me continually aware that writing is a great mystery is the experience of reading Melville.

★   ★   ★

One's first encounter with Melville is not usually in the books, *Typee* and *Omoo*, with which he began, but in *Moby-Dick*. It does not take long to realize that this is a writer whose relation to words is not so much mastery as it is a kind of hot intimacy in which the language will do anything he asks of it. He accosts you; he bends close to you to share a confidence; he wanders away from the point, distracted by a new half-formed idea; he falls away into silence as if stunned by the cost of his own discoveries. In "The Counterpane" chapter of *Moby-Dick* (where Ishmael's morning grogginess keeps him from distinguishing Queequeg's tattooed arm from the patchwork quilt under which both men have been sleeping), Melville manages to evoke a state of consciousness that is formidably difficult to represent—the limbo between sleep and wakefulness. But most of all, he proceeds through exuberant acts of association, by which "the great floodgates of the wonder-world [are] flung open":

> Nantucket! Take out your map and look at it. . . . Look at it—a mere hillock, and elbow of sand: all beach, without a background. There is more sand there than you would use in twenty years as a substitute for blotting paper. Some gamesome wights will tell you that they have to plant weeds there, they don't grow naturally; that they import Canada thistles; that they have to send beyond seas for a spile to stop a leak in an oil cask; that pieces of wood in Nantucket are carried about like bits of the true cross in Rome; that people there plant toadstools before their houses, to get under the shade in summer time; that one blade of grass makes an oasis, three blades in a day's walk a prairie; that they wear quicksand shoes, something like Laplander snow-shoes; that they are so

shut up, belted about, every way inclosed, surrounded, and made an utter island of by the ocean, that to their very chairs and tables small clams will sometimes be found adhering, as to the backs of sea turtles. But these extravaganzas only show that Nantucket is no Illinois.

Melville speaks in this passage as if he were returning with a report of an alien world to an uncomprehending reception party. He is looking for a way to represent a whole field of experience that is outside the capacity of the known language, so he scavenges among locally available metaphors—snowshoes, sunshades, the Cross—and assembles them into a picture that works indirectly, by the comparative logic of similes. The genius of the writing is its excess—what Walt Whitman had in mind when he claimed that his "elbows rest in sea-gaps," that he can "skirt sierras"—by which the likeness of toadstools and umbrellas is insolently asserted against the reader's dubiety. After the effort of holding together these antagonistic elements, the paragraph concludes with a sentence that stops the whole adventure abruptly like an adult putting an end to the high jinks of a child. This is a style that never becomes grave, but is always willing to make a joke of itself.

Reading backward and forward in Melville's work from the great center of *Moby-Dick*, one discovers that this exuberance is the other side of panic. When Melville writes with "the condor's quill," he covers great tracts with his Whitmanesque scrawl (the whale's "elevated hump [is] sun-dried as a dromedary's in the desert") and takes joy in breaking up what some critics nowadays call the "prison-house" of received language. But he cannot always maintain the almost manic defiance which the work of demolition requires. When he is taut and driven, like Ahab, we feel his love of language as an instrument of his will; when he slackens, we recognize his hatred of its limits, which is a different expression of the same fervor to be free within it. He knows the psychic costs of this rhythm, and gives us characters who are debilitated by it, such as Dr. Long Ghost in *Omoo*, who tells outrageous stories with "the real juice of sound," but when the telling is done, droops into a kind of withdrawal depression. Named for his appearance of spectral lankiness, Long Ghost is not so much lean as bony, an addict whose consumption (of drink, sex, stories) comes in bursts and confers no health.

The early Melville is, in something like this way, a greedy writer unable to resist the next synonym. Like his contemporary Whitman, he is drawn into an accretive style that issues catalogues. "What a sorry set of round-shouldered, spindle-shanked, crane-necked varlets" do "civilized men appear" when they walk naked among the beautiful Typees, for whom

> there were no foreclosures of mortgages, no protested notes, no bills payable, no debts of honor . . . no assault and battery attorneys, to foment discord . . . no beggars; no debtors' prisons; no proud and hard-hearted nabobs in Typee; or to sum up all in one word—no Money!

This exuberant inventory of absences forecasts Henry James's more famous list, presented thirty years later in his book on Hawthorne, of the liberating deficiencies of American life:

> No State, in the European sense of the word, and indeed barely a specific national name. No sovereign, no court, no

personal loyalty, no aristocracy, no church, no clergy, no army, no diplomatic service, no country gentlemen, no palaces, no castles, nor manors, nor old country-houses, nor parsonages, nor thatched cottages nor ivied ruins; no cathedrals, nor abbeys, nor little Norman churches; no great Universities nor public schools—no Oxford, nor Eton, nor Harrow; no literature, no novels, no museums, no pictures, no political society, no sporting class—no Epsom nor Ascot!

Until his late writings, Melville never relinquished the privilege of cataloguing. The prospect of summing "up all in one word" can never really become a wanted efficiency for any writer—it is a suicidal desire—and yet it is also always a theoretical goal. The few times it happens in Melville there is a kind of death in the act of summation.

In the early books, despite the pressures for sanitizing that are hard for an ambitious young writer to resist, Melville does not really restrain his language when it starts to run away from him. He does step outside the early narratives, and reports the debaucheries ("an abandoned voluptuousness I dare not attempt to describe") from a decent distance, playing the double game of attracting his reader by promising excitement and then recommending shame. But the more interesting way that Melville steers between his obligation of propriety and his drive to convey pleasure is to charge his prose with an erotic intensity that is hidden in submerged metaphors that the reader must tease to the surface.

When, in *Typee*, we enter the warm and liquid region of Nukuheva, we are invited privately to expose the sex of the language: we approach "by a narrow entrance, flanked on either side by two small twin islets which soar conically," beyond which the land "insensibly swells." A little later, in *Omoo*, the winds blow "like a woman roused, fiercely, but still warmly, in our faces," and the real girls perform a dance that promises, in the undulation of their collective outline, still more delicious openings and closings: "they pant hard and fast, a moment or two; and then, just as the deep flush is dying away from their faces, slowly recede, all round; thus enlarging the ring." The very landscape is tumescent, the trees "spreading overhead a dark, rustling vault, groined with boughs, and studded here and there with the ripened spheres, like gilded balls," and sometimes Melville's mind drifts to a ghostly whale ship that is said to be tacking off "Buggerry Island or the Devil's-Tail Peak."

There is a promiscuous delight in this language that is somewhere between the aphrodisiac pleasure of remembered sex and the almost carnal pleasure that Melville takes in the sheer virtuosity of his linguistic inventions. All phenomena become occasions for saving the physical texture of common experience from conventional description: (winter cold at sea) "any man could have undergone amputation with great ease, and helped to take up the arteries himself"; (buttons) a favorite prank in *White-Jacket* is for one sailor to snip off another's buttons as they stand at night on deck—permanent prunings, Melville says, since "there is no spontaneous vegetation in buttons." This is the impish Melville who loves to awaken our attention to the ordinary, like Picasso making handlebars into goat's horns or a child's toy car into a monkey.

More often, though, he does the reverse, holding strange and frightening things within reach of the reader's imagination by linking them to the familiar. At the apocalyptic end of *Moby-Dick*, after the white whale dives, the "cedar chips of the wrecks danced round and round, like the grated nutmeg in a swiftly stirred bowl of punch." Fear in Melville is never allowed to dissipate into the exotic or the remote.

Language, then, is a pleasure field, but also a problem. It is always slipping back into convention or evaporating into abstraction. In trying to rescue it from the deadening weight of culture, Melville tries to convert it from an inheritance into an invention. This is why, in *Redburn*, the little glass ship—a relic from his father's days as a world-traveling collector—reverberates symbolically in all his writing. The young narrator wants both to possess and to smash it; he is divided between a solemn reverence (which sometimes carries Melville's prose over the edge into pontification) and an antic fury that is really the same as young Redburn's desire to wreck the glass and have done with it.

This sort of productive anger, coiled within Melville's style, is also one of his themes. It is usually aimed, and sometimes released, at arrogant figures of power—like inherited language itself—whom Melville wants to drag back from their imperial aloofness into the world of human suffering. Such a desire overcomes the sailor-narrator of *White-Jacket* when, arraigned at the mast to receive an undeserved flogging, he bores his eyes into the boatswain's mate who stands "curling his fingers through the *cat*," and beyond him, into the indifferent Captain Claret:

> The Captain stood on the weather-side of the deck. Sideways ... was the opening of the lee-gangway, where the side ladders are suspended in port. Nothing but a slight of sinnate-stuff served to rail in this opening, ... and, though he was a

large, powerful man, it was certain that a sudden rush against
him, along the slanting deck, would infallibly pitch him head-
foremost into the ocean . . .

These computations are reported with a surveyor's precision,
and there is a clue here to why Melville almost always writes with
great tactility: the geography of the ship requires the reader's
shut-eyed concentration if it is to be accurately envisioned. There
can be no approximations or merely decorative metaphors in such
writing; it has to be serviceable as a guide to a strange place. But
in the next sentence Melville wants also to convey the storm in
the young sailor's mind, which is as obscure as the deck is lucid:

My blood seemed clotting in my veins; I felt icy cold at the
tips of my fingers, and a dimness was before my eyes. But
through that dimness the boatswain's mate, scourge in hand,
loomed like a giant, and Captain Claret, and the blue sea
seen through the opening of the gangway, showed with an
awful vividness. . . . [T]he thing that swayed me to my purpose was not altogether the thought that Captain Claret was
about to degrade me, and that I had taken an oath with my
soul that he should not. No, I felt my man's manhood so
bottomless within me, that no word, no blow, no scourge of
Captain Claret could cut me deep enough for that. I but
swung to an instinct in me—the instinct diffused through all
animated nature, the same that prompts even a worm to turn
under the heel. Locking souls with him, I meant to drag
Captain Claret from this earthly tribunal of his to that of
Jehovah, and let Him decide between us. No other way could
I escape the scourge.

The sequence of symptoms—clotting, cold, dimness—moves us from the external scene of confrontation into the internal landscape of mind, and then out again to the wide world of "all animated nature," where sanction for rage is to be found. Then, repossessing the whole of creation by dipping his pen into "Vesuvius' crater as an inkstand," Melville launches himself into the declamatory voice that will be heard in the "Knights and Squires" chapters of *Moby-Dick*:

> Nature has not implanted any power in man that was not meant to be exercised at times, though too often our powers have been abused. The privilege, inborn and inalienable, that every man has, of dying himself, and inflicting death upon another, was not given to us without a purpose. These are the last resources of an insulted and unendurable existence.

This meditation on the fragility of human structures (the Captain, in all his martial pomp, can be swept away by a lunging sailor) moves rapidly from the nautical to the personal to the oracular, each voice prescribed by literary precedents from which Melville borrows. This kind of stylistic prowling is one of the features of his prose that give it both its protomodernist and its cluttered, seventeenth-century quality. We are approaching here the symphonic texture of *Moby-Dick*, in which the narrative voice darts back and forth (sometimes within contiguous sentences) between the elevated and the vernacular, or disappears entirely into a choral burst. Sudden shifts of focus and intonation, the illogical ubiquity of Melville's narrators (Ishmael is somehow present in Ahab's cabin when the Captain is alone), and above all the refusal of the prose to settle into any steady pattern mark its fidelity to the fluidity of consciousness.

White-Jacket is on the verge of artistic maturity, which for Melville does not mean refinement but, rather, a boundless versatility. His narrators continually scan the repository of experience as stored in books, and pick out elements here and there with which to construct new voices and new meanings. "Books!" says Stubb, with "the Massachusetts calendar, and Bowditch's navigator, and Daboll's arithmetic" in mind, "you lie there; the fact is, you books must know your places. You'll do to give us the bare words and facts, but we come in to supply the thoughts." Melville's favored sources are Shakespeare for rhythms (most famously in Ahab's soliloquies) and the Bible for phrases, which he likes to situate in unlikely contexts. In *Omoo*, when he wants to expose a Tahitian boy as a male whore, he borrows a phrase from Paul's Epistle to the Corinthians: "He was, alas! as sounding brass and a tinkling cymbal; one of those who make no music unless the clapper be silver." The allusive range is wide; *Omoo* echoes not only scripture but also Milton in its concluding sentence ("all before us was the wide Pacific"), and *Moby-Dick* pays homage to acquisitive writers like Burton and Browne. *White-Jacket*, as its modern editors say, is a book of "extensive pillages" (the narrow escape from flogging may owe something to a newspaper account published in the 1830s); but whenever Melville borrows, he breaks the hold of his source and transforms it into an occasion for free meditation.

This way of dealing with inheritance—to acknowledge and master it—is a literary answer to the social and psychological problem Melville felt as the fallen scion of a once elevated family. Melville's father, whose own father had been a Revolutionary War hero, had failed in business and, by the early 1830s, had lost virtually everything, including his sanity. Among the most deeply felt pages in Melville's work are those describing Redburn's shame when he is unable to pay for his steamboat ticket, or the mockery he endures when he attempts, in his Sunday finery, to visit the Captain in his cabin. These moments of embarrassment involve a stinging sense of disproportion between his inherited language (not only verbal but also the languages of gesture and demeanor) and the facts of his fallen condition. The sound of his own voice makes him feel shriveled and half dead, as if a superannuated culture is speaking through him like a ghost through a medium.

What Melville's young men invariably discover at sea is the arbitrariness and limit of their previous idiom. It always fails them quickly, and in the ensuing confusion they grasp for new stabilities. Redburn learns, with the capering delight of a child who has discovered his musical gift, about *"passing a gammoning, reeving a Burton, strapping a shoe-block, clearing a foul hawse,* and innumerable other intricacies." Although this flood of new terminology alerts us to the thinness of our own lexicon, and to the fact that it can always be replenished and enlarged, it does not really satisfy Melville's craving for an experience outside the limits of language. Even the most circumscribed vocabularies can be invaded by new signifiers without altering the fundamental provincialism of the system—as when Bildad and Peleg, the Quaker owners of the *Pequod,* assess the value of Queequeg. At first he is nothing more than a mottled savage (whose name they garble into "Quohog" and "Hedgehog") looking to go to sea. But when they notice the deadly accuracy with which he throws a harpoon, they scramble to sign him up. Yet nothing has really changed in their way of apprehending the world. They have simply shifted him among categories already fixed in their minds—from an ominous savage to a proficient killer of whales.

Throughout the sea fiction, Melville tries to break out of this oppressive totality of language. When Tommo jumps ship in *Typee* it is to escape the hypocrisy of a captain who speaks with "paternal solicitude for the welfare of his crew" but whose actual practice is cruel. Tommo glimpses paradise when he encounters in the Typee valley "a boy and girl, slender and graceful," with whom no linguistic connection is possible, but with whom he "speaks" through a kind of improvised charade. This is for Melville the flicker of a prelapsarian world; he thinks of the fall much as we have come (under the sway of writers from Emerson to Lacan) to think of it—as a fall into language. The whole problem, certainly an old problem, is to climb out of language, to use it to get beyond itself, to find, as Whitman put it, a language "fann'd by the breath of nature."

In the pantomime world of *Typee* it sometimes seems that Melville has found such a natural language. Ignorant of and indifferent to the traces of their own history, the Typees have their Stonehenge, ancient mysterious terraces with "no inscriptions, no sculpture, no clue, by which to conjecture its history: nothing but the dumb stones," which they casually attribute to the gods. And if they have virtually no sense of the past, they have an equally small sense of the future; they are not confined, as Melville the Westerner feels himself to be, in a pinched moment called the present, and so they have no impulse to record themselves, or to question their ancestors, or to admonish their successors. In Typee, Fayaway's "labial melody" is enough.

A siren whose voice does no work of denotation, Fayaway only beckons and soothes; her companionship makes life "little else than an often interrupted and luxurious nap." And yet Melville eventually feels himself less liberated than trapped. Her dispensed pleasures are numbing; it is not the fear of rumored cannibalism that drives him away, but his sense that his self-consciousness is being exquisitely killed: "Forgetful . . . of [his] own situation," he finds that "over all the landscape there reigned the most hushed repose, which I almost feared to break lest, like the enchanted gardens in the fairy tale, a single syllable might dissolve the spell." The force of *Typee* is its account of how this silence finally becomes unbearable.

It is in *Omoo* (by comparison to *Typee*, a queasy, anxious book) that Melville first fully exposes what he calls the "fatal embrace" between Western and Pacific cultures. *Omoo* contains masterful miniature accounts of the dynamics of colonial domination—the entrepreneurship of Zeke and Shorty (the Yankee and Cockney partners who try to make a go of it as farmers in Polynesia), the portraits of natives who, like the Hawaiian chief who advertises himself as "the living tomb of Captain Cook's big toe," learn to emulate their new masters in treating the world as a storehouse of profitable opportunities. And it puts an early end to Melville's fantasy that he can step outside his own corrupting culture. With all his revulsion for hypocrisy (which will reach highest pitch in the portrait of the oily clergyman Falsegrave in *Pierre*) he acknowledges in *Omoo* that the crafty mediation of language between self and object is an indispensable pleasure. There is a more powerful sexual allure in a verbal Tahitian girl named Ideea than in mute Fayaway:

"Ah, Ideea, mickonaree oeee?" the same as drawling out—
"By the by, Miss Ideea, do you belong to the church?"

"Yes, me mickonaree," was the reply.

But the assertion was at once qualified by certain reservations; so curious, that I can not forbear their relation.

"Mickonaree *ena*" (church member *here*), exclaimed she, laying her hand upon her mouth, and a strong emphasis on the adverb. In the same way, and with similar exclamations, she touched her eyes and hands. This done, her whole air changed in an instant; and she gave me to understand, by unmistakable gestures, that in certain other respects she was not exactly a "mickonaree." In short, Ideea was

> *"A sad good Christian at the heart—*
> *A very heathen in the carnal part."*

By assigning (with a nicely pedantic footnote) the quoted lines to the Augustan poet Alexander Pope, Melville makes a little gesture at defending his propriety in telling this vignette. But he will not give up to his own censoriousness the very pleasures for which Ideea giggles and preens: the duplicity, deviousness, and irrepressible seductiveness of words.

By this early point in his development, Melville has fully considered a view of language not far from the postmodernist view: language as a contingent system whose rules define a game from which the innocent are excluded. Any gestures of connection to a transcendent absolute are likely to be dishonest or naive, and once one is in the game, it is virtually impossible to get out. This, I think, is why *Moby-Dick* begins not with the narrative but with the "extracts"—collections of words that do not disclose anything about whaleness ("Leviathan is the one creature in the world which must remain unpainted to the last") but only about the categories (legal, epic, poetic, physiological, sporting, religious) through which people have thought and talked about whales.

Melville has, in other words, discovered modernity. But he never rests easy with its skeptic relativism. He reports as a kind of desperate witness to (and prophet of) what it is like to live in a state of relentless suspicion toward appearances—or, more radically, in the certainty that appearances are all one can know. In this mood, which is more and more his governing state of mind, he never allows the present constitution of language to achieve the status of an axiom or an unrevisable truth. He prefers, in *White-Jacket*, to show the making of an aphorism rather than to avail himself of those already made; after the cook on a man-of-war has prepared the day's meal, he waits for the verdict of the taster, who is an officer of forbidding discretion in a world where "the Lords may be said to be tasters to the commons":

> But as all the meat is not inspected, and the cook may select what piece he pleases for inspection, the test is by no means a thorough one. A picked and pounded bit of the breast is not a fair specimen of a radically tough goose.

The moral of this little exemplum (the alliterative last sentence is worthy of Benjamin Franklin, whom Melville ridicules in *Israel Potter*) has a self-parodying air; but its serious work is to make the reader aware of the prehistory of a manufactured proverb.

Melville's instinct is more and more to deprive language of its air of authority by disrupting it at every level—even to the extent of repeating a characteristic syntactical error and (in the relatively

17

relaxed atmosphere of nineteenth-century grammatical practice) leaving it uncorrected: he typically says of Ahab, who is studying his charts, that "while thus employed, the heavy pewter lamp suspended in chains over his head, continually rocked . . . [and] threw shifting gleams and shadows upon" him. Invented epigrams and dangling participles are parts of Melville's improvisational style, but more remarkable is the work of continually generating new symbols. Under the pressure of his imagination, the Liverpool docks become more "stirring monuments" to human heroism than the "hermit obelisks of Luxor"; the monkey rope becomes a metaphor for the "Siamese connexion" between mutually dependent men; the tryworks furnish a smoking vision of hell.

Such disruption of normative language is most brilliantly carried off in Melville's great story "Bartleby, the Scrivener," about a copyist in a law office who begins as a no-trouble worker but one day unaccountably stops working. When asked to do a job, any job, he simply replies, "I would prefer not." Here a single word— the half-deferential, half-defiant verb "prefer"—creates a disturbance in the rote world of the lawyer and his scriveners, then becomes an affront and, finally, a contagion:

> "Say now you will help to examine papers to-morrow or next day: in short, say now that in a day or two you will begin to be a little reasonable:—say so, Bartleby."
>
> "At present I would prefer not to be a little reasonable," was his mildly cadaverous reply. . . .
>
> "*Prefer not*, eh?" gritted Nippers—"I'd *prefer* him, if I were you, sir," addressing me—"I'd *prefer* him; I'd give him preferences, the stubborn mule! What is it, sir, pray, that he *prefers* not to do now?"

Bartleby moved not a limb.

"Mr. Nippers," said I, "I'd prefer that you would withdraw for the present." . . .

As Nippers, looking very sour and sulky, was departing, Turkey blandly and deferentially approached.

"With submission, sir," said he, "yesterday I was thinking about Bartleby here, and I think that if he would but prefer to take a quart of good ale every day, it would do much towards mending him, and enabling him to assist in examining his papers."

"So you have got the word too," said I, slightly excited.

"With submission, what word, sir?" asked Turkey . . .

"I would prefer to be left alone here," said Bartleby, as if offended at being mobbed in his privacy.

"*That's* the word, Turkey," said I—"*that's* it."

"Oh, *prefer*? oh yes—queer word. I never use it myself. But, sir, as I was saying, if he would but prefer—"

"Turkey," interrupted I, "you will please withdraw."

"Oh certainly, sir, if you prefer that I should."

This little inset stage-piece builds its humor on the oafish ignorance of the players. I suspect that Melville must have seen early vaudeville performances in the New York theater that we would recognize as ancestors of the Abbott and Costello "who's on first" routine, where laughter is provoked by what seems the stupidity of men who cannot hear the very words they are using. But it is a nervous laughter, because no reader of "Bartleby" can fail to recognize the insidious ability of language to infiltrate speech without the speaker, in any conscious sense, knowing it.

"Prefer" is a grating word because it rubs against the language of Wall Street, suggesting the heightened politeness of the bitterly obedient servant whose only recourse against the master is to force him to drop his pretense of comradeship and to acknowledge his mastery. Like toilet water sprinkled on a dead man, the word does not cover the bad smell. The very sound of it torments Nippers and Turkey, the two Dickensian clerks who work alongside Bartleby and whose rebellions (insensible twitchings and private drinking binges) are barely conscious. It is a reproachful word from the past, suggesting genteel deference, but what it really does (which "I will not" or simply "No" would not do) is to throw the burden of action onto the man who has posed the question. With an unwitting presentiment of a political method of great importance in the coming century—nonviolent disobedience— the lawyer reflects that "nothing so aggravates an earnest person as a passive resistance." Bartleby's "prefer" forces him to consider, rather than to assume, the reasonableness of his request—to recognize that he has not asked a question at all, but has issued a command, and that behind the decorous facade of language lies naked power. Bartleby is being asked to expend his life in mindless submission to what the lawyer calls "common usage," and the word "prefer" compels everyone, including the mystified reader, to recognize this. It is a break in the customary language that reveals how appallingly unbroken is the rest of the structure.

There is, however, still a counterthrust in Melville's mature work that resists his own darkest insights into this imprisonment by language. This is the side of him that seems overwrought and even childish to certain fastidious readers; the side that Hawthorne saw when he remarked that he "will never rest until he gets hold of a definite belief." His prose attains its surpassing emotional power not finally because of its shrewdness about its own contingency, not even because of its sensuality or symbol-making prowess, but because it continues to resist the pressure from his intellect to abandon the idea—and the images—of transcendence. Melville knew that this kind of heart loyalty, held against corrosive internal doubt, can become a pathetic commitment, as it does in the case of Pierre, whose composure collapses when his belief is revealed to be groundless. But when belief is purged of vulgarity and sentiment—as it is in *The Encantadas*, when the hideously abandoned Chola widow, in order not to sink into solitary madness, scores a hollow reed with notches to mark the passing days—it justifies Melville's own homage: "Humanity, thou strong thing, I worship thee, not in the laurelled victor, but in this vanquished one."

At least until *The Confidence-Man*, there are sublime moments of such loyalty in Melville, when we feel that he has dampened all the competitive noise and actually overhears what Emerson called the conspiracy of nature with spirit "to emancipate us." This speech of nature, which, according to Emerson's faith, is "not fancied by some poet, but stands in the will of God," is recorded by Melville only in snatches and fragments, as in the "Grand Armada" chapter of *Moby-Dick*, or when Redburn contemplates the sea:

> As I looked at it so mild and sunny, I could not help calling to mind my little brother's face, when he was sleeping an infant in the cradle. It had just such a happy, careless, innocent look; and every happy little wave seemed gamboling about like a thoughtless little kid in a pasture; and seemed to look up in your face as it passed, as if it wanted to be patted and caressed. They seemed all live things with hearts

in them, that could feel; and I almost grieved, as we sailed
in among them, scattering them under our broad bows in
sun-flakes, and riding over them like a great elephant among
lambs. But what seemed perhaps the most strange to me of
all, was a certain wonderful rising and falling of the sea; I do
not mean the waves themselves, but a sort of wide heaving
and swelling and sinking all over the ocean. It was something
I can not very well describe; but I know very well what it
was, and how it affected me. It made me almost dizzy to look
at it; and yet I could not keep my eyes off it, it seemed so
passing strange and wonderful.

More often, the idea of divinity is hinted as a haunting possibility that can be glimpsed in certain arresting images—like the
swinging lamp in Jonah's cabin (as told by Father Mapple in
Moby-Dick) that remains "infallibly straight" as the ship pitches,
and makes "obvious the false, lying levels among which it hung."
For Melville, the most promising way to break through the "false,
lying" opacity of human language to the "linked correspondences"
of perception and expression is to drive away the notion that
words stand in a fixed relation to the phenomena they represent.
In attacking this allegorical idea—which he recognizes as a prop
of every culture—he does not falter even when denotation gives
way to a kind of atavistic chant. Here is Stubb urging on the
oarsmen in his boat:

"Start her, start her, my men! Don't hurry yourselves; take
plenty of time—but start her; start her like thunder claps,
that's all," cried Stubb, spluttering out the smoke as he
spoke. "Start her, now; give 'em the long and strong stroke,

Tashtego. Start her, Tash, my boy—start her, all; but keep cool, keep cool—cucumbers is the word—easy, easy—only start her like grim death and grinning devils, and raise the buried perpendicular out of their graves, boys—that's all. Start her!"

"Woo-hoo! Wa-hee!" screamed the Gay-Header in reply . . .

But his wild screams were answered by others quite as wild. "Kee-hee! Kee-hee!" yelled Daggoo, straining forwards and backwards on his seat, like a pacing tiger in his cage.

"Ka-la! Koo-loo!" howled Queequeg, as if smacking his lips over a mouthful of Grenadier's steak. And thus with oars and yells the keels cut the sea.

This language is irrational not just in its frenzy and sublinguistic cries but in its attack upon itself: it recommends the coolness of grinning devils and demands instant action without haste. In passages like this, Melville is abandoning the "systematized exhibition" of experience and stretches his words to a miraculous thinness, a translucence that might let the divine light through. Barely held back from disappearing into pure sound, the language is being pushed toward the condition of music, where there is no stable foreground or background and no possibility of paraphrase or reductive translation. The words shimmer like the "visible surface of the Sperm Whale":

Almost invariably it is all over obliquely crossed and re-crossed with numberless straight marks in thick array, something like those in the finest Italian line engravings. But these marks do not seem to be impressed upon this isinglass

substance [of the blubber], but seem to be seen through it,
as if they were engraved upon the body itself.

In the whale the distinction between depth and surface is elusive
if not illusory, in the same way that Nantucket, seen through the
wonderful romp of "extravaganzas," is "all beach, without a background."

Of the many Melvillean figures who enter this undifferentiated
landscape—which is both a heaven and a hell—the one who is
introduced most violently into it is the black cabin boy in *Moby-
Dick*, Pip. Thrown out of his rushing whaleboat into the open sea,
he finds, as the boats speed away from him after their prey, that
his "ringed horizon began to expand around him miserably." In
his literally unspeakable solitude he finds that "strange shapes of
the unwarped primal world glided to and fro before his passive
eyes," and his language is virtually obliterated. If "he saw God's
foot upon the treadle of the loom, and spoke it," his expression
of what he has seen after he is rescued (by sheerest chance)
shrinks to a schoolboy's conjugation: "I look, you look, he looks,
we look, ye look, they look."

In this extraordinary moment Melville actually inhabits the
mind of one whose identity has been sucked out of him ("Pip's
missing," the boy says to Ahab) and is reduced to the expression
of a pure relativism. It may be the most brilliant evocation of the
black experience of abandonment in American literature until
Ralph Ellison's *Invisible Man*. To read it is to feel something of
the way one feels when watching a stroke victim laboriously regain
lost speech—but in this case the lesson, we know, can never advance beyond metronomic rehearsal of the verb. There is a terrible blockage here; it is the realization of the darkest possibility

that follows from Melville's relentless attack on all culturally formed contingencies that pass for truth. It is also a surrender of his cherished ideal of a language with no prescribed grammar, where invention and whim range free, but which might still somehow be able to link one mind intimately with another. This was never an easy thing to imagine, and after *Moby-Dick* Melville all but gives it up.

There are a few subsequent moments, especially in the title piece of *The Piazza Tales*, when some of Melville's former joy in the expressive power of language is briefly restored—the power, as in *Moby-Dick*, to make palpable the "crystal goblets of Persian sherbet" as a metaphor for equatorial spring nights at sea. In such moments we get a cascade of images that push prose to its limits:

> Beneath swaying fir-boughs petted by no season, but still green in all, on I journeyed—my horse and I; on, by a deep flume clove through snowy marble, vernal-tinted, where freshet eddies had, on each side, spun out empty chapels in the living rock; on, where Jacks-in-the-pulpit, like their Baptist namesake, preached but to the wilderness; on, where a huge, cross-grain block, fern-bedded, showed where, in forgotten times man after man had tried to split it, but lost his wedges for his pains—which wedges yet rusted in their holes; on, where, ages past, in step-like ledges of a cascade, skull-hollow pots had been churned out by ceaseless whirling of a flint stone—ever wearing, but itself unworn; on, by wild rapids pouring into a secret pool, but soothed by circling there

awhile, issued forth serenely; on, to less broken ground, and by a little ring, where, truly, fairies must have danced, or else some wheel-tire been heated—for all was bare; still on, and up, and out into a hanging orchard . . .

As with certain passages in *Moby-Dick* that want to break out of the paragraphs and assemble themselves into blank verse, the incantatory rhythms of "The Piazza" might fall better into lines than sentences. But such effusions grow rare; by the time of *The Confidence-Man* Melville is writing denuded sentences whose short dependent clauses are held together by weak strings of commas:

> At an interesting point of the narration, and at the moment when, with much curiosity, indeed, urgency, the narrator was being questioned upon that point, he was, as it happened, altogether diverted both from it and his story, by just then catching sight of a gentleman who had been standing in sight from the beginning, but, until now, as it seemed, without being observed by him.

This sentence has a certain organized tidiness; it is grammatically competent (well formed in the Chomskyan sense), but it stands cryptically at the start of a new chapter, and in the whirling context of the larger narrative it is not clear whose is the curiosity or the urgency or the interest. We do not know if the crippled Guinea, whom the "narrator" has been defending, is a white impostor in blackface; or if the man with the wooden leg, who tells a bawdy story, is a quick-change artist who returns to revile the "diverted" storyteller; or even if *The Confidence-Man* itself is a drama played by a single actor or a whole troupe. This is not the "cunning" and "feline" madness of *Moby-Dick* but the linguistic equivalent of a brain-dead person having the air and blood forced by a machine through the old passageways. There is motion in such sentences, but no life left.

The Confidence-Man marks a collapse of Melville's will to believe from which he would never entirely recover, a breakdown adumbrated in *Pierre* and in his great novella *Benito Cereno*, which is Melville's most punishing exhibition of how impenetrable a mind can become when entrapped in a fixed cultural vocabulary. But *Benito Cereno* is also an announcement of dread at the vertigo that sets in when the old structure explodes. The obtuse Captain Delano has been unable to see, despite many hints, that the Spanish slave ship which he boards has been taken over by its slaves and that the black "valet" Babo is controlling the Spanish captain like a puppeteer. Even as Delano departs, and the terrified Spaniard leaps over the bulwarks into the rowboat as it shoves off, he remains convinced that white over black is the only conceivable order of the world; and even when Babo, with knife drawn, leaps after the Spaniard, Delano can only imagine that the blade is aimed at himself. When the truth of the matter finally dawns on him, Melville reports his "revelation" in a carefully disfigured sentence: "Not Captain Delano, but Don Benito, the black, in leaping into the boat, had intended to stab."

Sorting out the elements of this twisted sentence into the ordinary English sequence of subject, verb, object is hard work. Yet even after we have parsed it, we are left with the feeling that we have relinquished one arbitrary structure of interpretation for another. Delano, who once thought that whites ruled over blacks, now sees that blacks rule over whites. This is all he has learned. Of the horrors that lie behind both white supremacy and black vengeance he remains entirely innocent.

After such ferocious attacks on the fond idea that truth might be accessible through language, it is all the more remarkable that in his self-consciously final work, *Billy Budd*, published posthumously in 1924 (it was found among his possessions upon his death in 1891), Melville comes closest to achieving the transcendence he had given up on. After long silence, he returned to a prose that is neither frolicsome nor spent but that reaches a repose quite unlike anything he had achieved before. *Billy Budd* is the work of a diminished imagination, not in the sense of attenuation or decline, but in new reserve and acquiescence. "No great and enduring volume can ever be written on the flea," Melville had said in *Moby-Dick*, but now he reflects that "passion in its profoundest, is not a thing demanding a palatial stage whereon to play its part." After the blood-chilling moment when venomous Claggart, like Mephistopheles with his cane, taps Billy from behind to commend him for the mess he has made when his chowder runs on the deck, Melville says of *Billy Budd* that it is a drama provoked by "a man-of-war's man's spilled soup."

Yet it is a drama of immense power, at the center of which is the confrontation between "welkin-eyed" Billy, a "novice in the complexities of factitious life," and Claggart, "in whom was the mania of an evil nature" not susceptible to any of the explanations that the modern mind can muster—"not engendered by vicious training or corrupting books or licentious living, but born with him and innate." In a world where the language of "Holy Writ" has been discredited, Claggart is simply beyond explanation (modern critics have added frustrated homosexual desire to Melville's list); but when Claggart finishes his slander that Billy is making a mutiny, Melville does find a way to represent him in his priapic pride:

> . . . the accuser's eyes, removing not as yet from [Billy's] blue dilated ones, underwent a phenomenal change, their wonted rich violet color blurring into a muddy purple. Those lights of human intelligence, losing human expression, were gelidly protruding like the alien eyes of certain uncatalogued creatures of the deep. The first mesmeristic glance was one of serpent fascination; the last was as the paralyzing lurch of the torpedo fish.

Billy, whose "liability to a vocal defect" now afflicts him utterly, has really always been speechless in the sense of having no place in a world where language is the instrument of guile and irony. He takes no part in the speech that surrounds him, in which the ship's guns are blessed as "peacemakers," and officers talk elliptically of impressed men as those who have "entered His Majesty's service under another form than enlistment." Unfamiliar with "double meanings and insinuations of any sort," Billy is "illiterate, he could not read, but he could sing, and like the illiterate nightingale was sometimes the composer of his own song." When he sings, or when, in his last moment of life, he blesses Captain Vere with "words wholly unobstructed in the utterance," he expresses what Melville has tried all his life to release from the suffocating embrace of language: "the veritable unobstructed outcome of the innermost man." At all other times, Billy's stammer is his essence.

Billy Budd is the rapturous invention of an imagination both sustained and starved by the actuality of this world. In the end, Melville does not try to represent him with descriptive phrases or by reporting his spare words; instead, he coaxes an image of Billy out of clustered associations that evoke in the reader the idea of a bodiless being suddenly realized in flesh, an idea or principle that briefly achieves, or lapses into, incarnation. Billy cannot be designated by any fixed image; he can only be likened to others that may be passed before the reader's eyes. He is "something analogous to that of a rustic beauty transplanted from the provinces and brought into competition with the highborn dames of the court"; his face, when he is libeled by Claggart, is "like that of a condemned vestal priestess in the moment of being buried alive."

After Billy strikes out silently against his accuser, it is an agony for Vere to sacrifice him to the requirements of law and king. Vere stands "alone on the weather side of the quarter-deck," where Melville has placed himself—with his back to the possibility of transcendence. Even as he prepares to send Billy out of the world, Vere acknowledges his own imprisonment in a radically unsatisfying culture, and shares his most merciful officers' impulse to break free of it. After he rebukes them for the thought of mitigating the death sentence, and imagines on their behalf the chaos of private imperatives that would ensue, he delivers "of his own motion . . . the finding of the court to the prisoner." This scene Melville cannot bear to narrate. "There is no telling the sacrament," he explains, and like the great moment in *Benito Cereno* when the slave shaves his master with a honed razor, the events are kept offstage, left for us to imagine. Yet somehow, without dialogue or eyewitness description, the scene comes into being, as a faint vibration between the explanatory passages that surround it:

> The first to encounter Captain Vere in the act of leaving the compartment was the senior lieutenant. The face he beheld, for the moment one expressive of the agony of the strong, was to that officer, though a man of fifty, a startling revelation.

What is revealed to the startled lieutenant is "that the condemned one suffered less than he who mainly had effected the condemnation." The cabin scene in which Vere tells his beloved Billy that he must die cannot be written, but it is nevertheless heard. It is a pianissimo melody amid brute noise; we dare not breathe for fear of obscuring the tiny sublime sound with our own intolerable rasping. The untold sacrament has done its office, and Melville— even as he concludes that the only sounds audible in the cosmos are echoes of the human voice—has let us hear God.

2

Thoreau Faces Death

There is an unprovable story that when Thoreau was teaching school in Concord (a plum of a job after the 1837 financial crash), a school board member visited his class and reprimanded him for failing to cane his students. Thoreau walked back into the classroom, selected six students at random, and beat them vigorously. And then he quit. The story accords with Thoreau's spirit, if not necessarily with the facts, and there is a hint in it of his peculiar position in the American literary tradition. The better-known part of him is the gentle dissident who spent a night in Concord jail rather than pay the poll tax. But he had also a certain pursed-lipped sourness; out on the trail he was adept, as his biographer Robert Richardson has put it, at consuming wild berries that "were so tart it was a triumph to eat them."

Thoreau's was an unreconciled temperament. If he wrote reverently about nature, he was equally capable of writing about people with a shriveling disdain:

> One farmer says to me, "You cannot live on vegetable food
> solely, for it furnishes nothing to make bones with"; and so
> he religiously devotes a part of his day to supplying his system
> with the raw material of bones; walking all the while he talks
> behind his oxen, which, with vegetable-made bones, jerk him
> and his lumbering plough along in spite of every obstacle.

Thoreau would have something acerbic to say, in this spirit,
about his appearance in one of the black-jacketed volumes in the
uniform edition of American classics published by the Library of
America, for which he has been cut to the same size, bound in
the same cloth, and furnished with the same typeface and book-
mark ribbon as the other writers chosen for inclusion. Being pack-
aged as a worthy would make him uneasy, since among the great
figures of the American Renaissance he was the most suspicious,
arch, macabre. He was corrosively skeptical of all established
structures and quick to categorize other men even as he condemned them for having categorical minds. In his lapidary technique and ghoulish humor (in the "Higher Laws" chapter of
Walden he says that he is "strongly tempted to seize and devour
[a woodchuck] raw") he bore less resemblance to the earnest New
England "transcendentalists" than to the alien writer Emerson
called "the jingle man"—that is, to Poe.

Wounded by a sense of disfranchisement—the son of a pencil
maker, he was short of money most of his life—Thoreau was
always contemptuous of social organizations, even those that were
willing to include him. When he replied to the Harvard alumni
questionnaire by acknowledging that he was only marginally employed, he declined to be considered a charity case, and offered
advice to any of his classmates who might wish something more

valuable than money. Asked to join the Brook Farm communal experiment, he refused on the grounds that "I had rather keep bachelor's hall in hell than go to board in heaven." And when he traveled through New England in search of the receding wilderness, walking "across-lots," and following his compass and ignoring the fences and hedges that marked property lines, he saw nature as a great contaminated garden, and could seem oblivious of the plucky men who struggled to make a living from what nature supplied them.

No wonder that we hear so often of vessels which are becalmed off our coast, being surrounded a week at a time by floating lumber from the Maine woods. The mission of men there seems to be, like so many busy demons, to drive the forest all out of the country, from every solitary beaver swamp and mountain-side, as soon as possible.

The hovels of the cattle, he remarks, could be distinguished from those of the loggers only because they have no chimneys.

For the last twenty-four of his forty-five years, Thoreau kept a journal that ran to nearly two million words. Out of the more than forty volumes of what John L. O'Sullivan called "private interviews with nature," he fashioned two books that were published in his lifetime, A Week on the Concord and Merrimack Rivers and Walden. Through the efforts of friends, two more volumes, The Maine Woods and Cape Cod (which had appeared partially in magazines), and several collections of essays and letters were published posthumously. As a result, we think of Thoreau as a writer of books. But it is not clear that this is the way he wanted it to be. "I do not know," he wrote in his journal in 1852, "but thoughts written down thus in a journal might be printed in the same form to greater advantage—than if the related ones were brought together into separate essays. They are now allied to life—& are seen by the reader not to be far fetched."

The fact is that Thoreau did fetch his own words from afar—from back volumes of his journal—for both *A Week* and *Walden*, which are books more constructed than written, for which the writer has plagiarized himself. Thoreau lived at Walden Pond, in a cabin of his own construction (neighbors helped to raise the frame), for twenty-six months, beginning on July 4, 1845. While other New Englanders went on grand adventures—R. H. Dana to the open sea, Francis Parkman to the Northwest Territory—Thoreau remarked coyly that he had "traveled much in Concord."

His two years at the little pond outside the village have struck many readers as somehow comical, like a child camping in the backyard, bravely holding back urine until morning to avoid having to squat outdoors. He "sneaked back from Walden in the evening," says Harold Bloom, "to be fed dinner by Lidian Emerson." But these chastisements miss the point. Thoreau was not embarked on some Outward Bound test of manhood, yet where he

> lived was as far off as many a region viewed nightly by astronomers. We are wont to imagine rare and delectable places in some remote and more celestial corner of the system, behind the constellation of Cassiopeia's Chair, far from noise and disturbance. I discovered that my house actually had its site in such a withdrawn, but forever new and unprofaned, part of the universe.

Walden is the honest record of this self-exile. It is not an advertisement of competence or courage. Much of what he wrote in his journal while at Walden found its way, after many revisions, into the final version of the book, which was published in 1854. But the text as we know it also draws on earlier and later sources—notes he took on Staten Island years before; short, self-contained essays on what we would call the semiotics of clothing ("the head monkey at Paris puts on a traveller's cap, and all the monkeys in America do the same") that he had written out in the early 1840s. Thoreau was a craftsman who worked with self-quotation and shuffled words that had once been, in Wordsworth's phrase, "the spontaneous overflow of powerful feelings," but function later like modular blocks that can be placed in new relations with others composed in entirely discrete moods and moments.

There is, as a result, a certain technological quality to the writing that Thoreau supervised for publication, as if he anticipated the new compositional possibilities that have become available to us all through the word processor. In this sense he belongs to a tradition of esoteric virtuosity; there are puzzles and clues embedded in *Walden*, a book that bristles with jokes in several languages, and contains brilliant set pieces, such as the passage in which a wounded ant becomes Patroclus and his ferocious ally who avenges him by "gnawing at the near fore-leg of his enemy" becomes a formic Achilles.

A great deal of Thoreau's laborious artifice has been detailed by recent critics, but it was recognized already in his own time by his fellow transcendentalist Margaret Fuller. She wrote him a shrewd rejection note in response to an early submission he had sent to the *Dial*:

> Last night's second reading only confirms my impression from the first. The essay is rich in thoughts, and I should be pained not to meet it again. But then, the thoughts seem to me so out of their natural order, that I cannot read it through without pain. I never once felt myself in a stream of thought, but seem to hear the grating tools on the mosaic.

This is perhaps the most acute comment ever made about Thoreau. Its establishment of the "stream of thought" as the ideal of literary representation that eluded him predates William James's "stream of consciousness" by fifty years and Gertrude Stein by seventy-five. And when Fuller speaks of the pain she felt in both approaching and leaving Thoreau's prose, she has recognized in him a certain penal quality that is his genius and his limitation.

Thoreau inflicts a kind of punishment on his reader because he hated intellectual laziness. He hated it in the way that Harriet Beecher Stowe hated slavery. He forbids us to relax into any accustomed mental posture: "We wished," he writes in *Cape Cod*, "to associate with the ocean until it lost the pond-like look which it wears to a countryman." The point is to attack all received ideas and images until they disintegrate under the assault. *Walden* is a lethal work ("I had three pieces of limestone on my desk, but I was terrified to find that they required to be dusted daily, when the furniture of my mind was all undusted still, and I threw them out the window in disgust") that leaves no structure standing through which we may see, sense, or think the world as we had done before we read it. *Walden* is, in this sense, a very intolerant book.

Its Emersonian project of destruction proceeds through a prose style that moves almost mechanically back and forth between contradictory assertions. "Old people," Thoreau tells us, "did not know enough once, perchance, to fetch fresh fuel to keep the fire a-going; new people put a little dry wood under a pot, and are whirled around the globe with the speed of birds." But at the same time the idea of progress is one of the myths he wishes most urgently to discredit: "We are eager to tunnel under the Atlantic and bring the old world some weeks nearer to the new; but perchance the first news that will leak through into the broad, flapping American ear will be that the Princess Adelaide has the whooping cough."

Reading Thoreau is like walking a line held taut between two opposite-leaning posts. The prose retains its tension because of its internal antagonisms, which is why *Walden* has lately proven so attractive to the deconstructionists. Thoreau was not only a contradictory writer but a contradictory man—a conservationist who once burned down three hundred acres of woods by leaving a campfire undoused; a victim, according to some recent medical historians, of narcolepsy who proclaimed his commitment always to wake up with the sun. A man's "growth requires" that he "remember well his ignorance," he tells us, yet he sends this proposition into collision with another one equally authoritative: "Those who have not learned to read the ancient classics in the language in which they were written must have a very imperfect knowledge of the history of the human race." The building materials of rustic *Walden* are its aphorisms modeled on classical *sententiae*; it is a book that summons us back to ignorance even as it rebukes us for the very ignorance we are supposed to recover.

Beneath this vibration of contraries is a dreadful emptiness. The most cultivated and scholastic of the chief writers of the American Renaissance, Thoreau was ultimately a despiser of culture. He

faced an abyss of his own creating, I think—the specter of absolute self-reliance more radical than even Emerson contem-
plated. What Thoreau discovered was that language itself, in the
narrow sense of verbal vocabulary and in the wider sense of gesture and accoutrements, made him feel dead because it subjected
him to the worn and degraded inventions of other minds. We are
"like cowbirds and cuckoos, which lay their eggs in nests which
other birds have built, and cheer no traveller with their chattering
and unmusical notes." Thoreau wanted desperately to make his
own music, "to brag as lustily as Chanticleer in the morning,
standing on his roost, if only to wake my neighbors up." Without
the sound of his own voice, in the fullest proprietary sense, he
felt lost in the cacophony of culture and regarded himself as a
bloodless automaton.

Yet language was the human thing he most loved. One becomes
aware of this from the way he italicizes certain words like *auction*
and *malaria*, which carry, for him, not merely their conventional
contemporary meanings (a public competitive sale; a feverish disease) but also older etymological meanings (an increase; bad air),
resonances from the Latin and Italian which have become almost
inaudible beneath the parochial hum of culture. These ancient
meanings are precious to Thoreau, not because they confer upon
such words the dignity of age or require acts of archaeology from
the superior reader, but because they suggest a pure point of
locatable origin behind the process of linguistic change. Words,
for Thoreau, carry traces of God.

Walden, in this sense, is a redemptive book. It peels away the
layers of culture from everything it examines—words, dress,

social habits—because beneath them, Thoreau believes, lies some ultimate stability that exists outside time. He was less the modern writer than his contemporary Melville, who, though he shared Thoreau's quest for divinity in and through language, suspected that "by vast pains we mine into the pyramid; by horrible gropings we come to the central room; with joy we espy the sarcophagus; but we lift the lid—and no body is there!—appallingly vacant as vast is the soul of a man!"

Facing the prospect of such deserted ruins, Thoreau became what I would call a secret Catholic—the pilgrim who discovers and takes refuge in what he judges to be the one durable church in which the spirit of God has consented to be realized in human form. Of the members of Emerson's circle, only Orestes Brownson actually converted to Rome, but Thoreau, no less passionately, made a Church of his own words. "It is something to be able to paint a particular picture, or to carve a statue, and so to make a few objects beautiful; but it is far more glorious to carve and paint the very atmosphere and medium through which we look." Words themselves become objects of worship, which enable us "to apprehend . . . what is sublime and noble . . . by the perpetual instilling and drenching of the reality which surrounds us."

As *Walden* proceeds with this sanctifying fervor, it is written more and more as if its own purified vocabulary were literally the only words God has permitted to be left in the world. This kind of self-enclosure may be seen in the stunning chapter "The Village," which describes the Main Street of Concord as a complete digestive system, by which the traveler is ingested, passed, and excreted "out through the rear avenues." One can read this passage repeatedly without noticing the excremental metaphor, but once it is pointed out (as it was to me years ago by Joel Porte) the passage can never be read innocently again. Though it may certainly have precedents in Dante and Rabelais and others, Thoreau's own metaphoric invention now controls us utterly. Concord becomes a permanently clogged intestine, and his revulsion becomes our own. After reading "The Village" it is hard to visit Concord as a cheerful tourist—as unlikely as tapping one's foot to "Singin' in the Rain" after seeing *A Clockwork Orange*.

This passage, like many others among the most achieved in *Walden* and *A Week*, had first been written out years before in the journal, and was placed like an adjusted piece of masonry into a waiting slot in the book. Here, I think, we come to the heart of Thoreau's dilemma. The project of his books is to break down the structures that intervene between culture and nature: "If you stand right fronting and face to face to a fact, you will see the sun glimmer on both its surfaces, as if it were a cimeter, and feel its sweet edge dividing you through the heart and marrow, and so you will happily conclude your mortal career." But in the end this ecstatic suicide cannot be performed through highly conscious craftsmanship, which creates opaque, if impressive, new edifices.

The most moving moments in *Walden* are those where Thoreau recognizes this impasse:

> Though the woodchoppers have laid bare first this shore and then that, and the Irish have built their sties by it, and the railroad has infringed on its border, and the ice-men have skimmed it once, it is itself unchanged, the same water which my youthful eyes fell on; all the change is in me. It has not acquired one permanent wrinkle after all its ripples. . . . It struck me again to-night, as if I had not seen it almost daily

for more than twenty years,—Why, here is Walden, the same woodland lake that I discovered so many years ago; . . . it is the same liquid joy and happiness to itself and its Maker, ay, and it *may* be to me.

Thoreau speaks here of the lake as if he has puppied after it ("almost daily") like a shooed-away lover who will not give up; but the more devastating confession is that the aliveness that he had once known is slipping away. Thoreau's self-portrait in *Walden* belongs with Dreiser's portrait of Hurstwood in *Sister Carrie* and Hemingway's of Jake Barnes in *The Sun Also Rises*—men whose sensory capacities are failing. Through and against language, Thoreau tries to get these powers back.

Another way to put this is to say that death is the specter over Thoreau's work. Magnifying the death struggle of the red and black ants under a tumbler on his windowsill, he writes with efficient fascination about the "breast all torn away," the exposed vitals, "the still living heads . . . hanging on either side of" one ant "like ghastly trophies at his saddle-bow." In the harrowing first chapter of *Cape Cod* he walks the beach after a ship carrying Irish immigrants has run aground and broken up:

I saw many marble feet and matted heads as the cloths were raised, and one livid, swollen, and mangled body of a drowned girl,—who probably had intended to go out to service in some American family,—to which some rags still adhered, with a string, half concealed by the flesh, about its swollen neck; the coiled-up wreck of a human hulk, gashed by the rocks or fishes, so that the bone and muscle were exposed, but quite bloodless,—merely red and white,—with

wide-open and staring eyes, yet lustreless, dead-lights; or like
the cabin windows of a stranded vessel, filled with sand.

This kind of writing, posing as an aesthetic evaluation, is really
a test of Thoreau's capacity to keep from flinching as "the sweet
edge" of death cuts him "through the heart and marrow"—as
he had been cut years before by his brother's agonized death
from lockjaw. He presents, for his own strengthening, the image
of the

> men with carts busily collecting the sea-weed which the
> storm had cast up, and conveying it beyond the reach of the
> tide, though they were often obliged to separate fragments
> of clothing from it, and they might at any moment have
> found a human body under it. Drown who might, they did
> not forget that this weed was a valuable manure.

One is tempted to hear in this report the old intolerant voice
of the lemonish Thoreau, as if he is judging these scavengers for
disrespecting the dead. But I think the emotion here is closer to
envy than to disgust. These stoic New Englanders are part of the
natural cycle of things, salvaging the seaweed, preparing it for
market or their own use, undefeated by the prospect that each
new wave may wash up a new corpse and remind them of their
own mortality. Thoreau wants not to dismiss them, but to find a
way—despite all his contempt for the drudgery and thoughtless-
ness of their labor—to join them.

He wants, in other words, to be somehow immunized against
the fate of one

woman who had come over [from Ireland] before, but had left her infant behind for her sister to bring, [and who] came and looked into these boxes, and saw in one . . . her child in her sister's arms, as if the sister had meant to be found thus; and within three days after, the mother died from the effect of that sight.

Thoreau's writing is, in the final analysis, an effort to train himself to go on living after such a sight.

The finished books are the public testimonies of his survival. But his real self-therapy was his journal. It was published at the beginning of this century in a bulky edition, but is now being edited into a new clear text by a team of scholars at the Princeton University Press, who have included some material never before published—fragmentary remains of portions of the journal from which Thoreau tore out sheets for insertion into works in draft. In the Princeton edition we can see Thoreau's conception of the journal changing from a storehouse to be raided to an integral work in its own right. I would venture the prediction that Thoreau's reputation has not yet reached its peak, because we are only beginning to know the journal. As it emerges we shall recognize more and more his prescient formulations of what has become the leading intellectual problem of our time: the effort to move from the skeptical to the constructive mood; to come to terms with the discovery that rationality is just one in the infinite range of possible cultural performances; to remake a humane world when the human "sciences" seem devoted to exposing their own arbitrariness.

Thoreau's skepticism was no less stringent than our own. What he had that we are losing was the redemptive idea of nature. It is in the journals even more than in the great books of "natural history"—*A Week, Walden, The Maine Woods, Cape Cod*—that he takes us without stint to the experience of "fronting" nature. In the most careful study yet of the compositional relations between the journal and the books, H. Daniel Peck remarks that

> for Thoreau, the very act of making a "book" implied closure.
> . . . To make a book like *Walden* meant drawing a boundary
> around the experiences it describes . . . and it is precisely be-
> cause he did not have to think of his Journal as a text that
> he felt free to range between category and relation exactly
> as the power of paradigms, on the one hand, and the power
> of the world's images, on the other, moved him.

One sample from the extraordinary journal (from July 1851) will illustrate Peck's important point:

> Now I yearn for one of those old meandering dry uninhab-
> ited roads which lead away from towns—which lead us away
> from temptation, which conduct to the outside of earth—
> over its uppermost crust—where you may forget in what
> country you are travelling—where no farmer can complain
> that you are treading down his grass—no gentleman who has
> recently constructed a seat in the country that you are tres-
> passing—on which you can go off at half cock—and wave
> adieu to the village—along which you may travel like a pil-
> grim—going nowhither. Where travellers are not too often
> to be met. Where my spirit is free—where the walls & fences

are not cared for—where your head is more in heaven than your feet are on earth—which have long reaches—where you can see the approaching traveler half a mile off and be prepared for him—not so luxuriant a soil as to attract men—some root and stump fences which do not need attention—where travelers have no occasion to stop—but pass along and leave you to your thoughts— Where it makes no odds which way you face whether you are going or coming—whether it is morning or evening—mid-noon or mid-night— Where earth is cheap enough by being public. Where you can walk and think with least obstruction—there being nothing to measure progress by.

The exhilarating forward pressure of the open punctuation, the indifference to time, the ebullience of the Janus-faced traveler, all ensure that wherever we stop quoting from this passage, we have severed it from itself. Thoreau could not "walk and think with least obstruction" in the confines of a book. He was freest in his journal, and he knew, even as he made more than one literary monument out of it, that he was doing it a violence.

Reading Thoreau, whether in the spontaneous journal or in the finished books, one feels accused of hoarding comforts. Among the strongest reactions I have ever witnessed in a student was during a class on *Walden* when one of my undergraduates, a daughter of Korean immigrants, protested almost to the point of tears that she valued her clothes, her furniture, her *things*, and that she resented this man for trying to take this capacity for pleasure away from her. "It is desirable that a man be clad so simply that he can lay his hands on himself in the dark, and that he live in all respects so compactly and preparedly, that if an enemy take the town, he can, like the old philosopher, walk out the gate empty-handed without anxiety." My student did not want to hear that. Her protest was heartfelt because Thoreau had reached her, as we say, where she lives.

He is, despite all the barricades he erected around himself, an irresistible writer; to read him is to feel wrenched away from the customary world and delivered into a place we fear as much as we need. Midway on his hike toward Mount Katahdin, he accepts a proffered drink from a backwoodsman and finds that "it was as if we sucked at the very teats of Nature's pine-clad bosom." Then, in words of wonderful pungency, he gives us (and himself) the full flavor of the drink: it tasted of

> the sap of all Millinocket botany commingled,—the topmost, most fantastic, and spiciest sprays of the primitive wood, and whatever invigorating and stringent gum or essence it afforded steeped and dissolved in it,—a lumberer's drink, which would acclimate and naturalize a man at once,—which would make him see green, and, if he slept, dream that he heard the wind sough among the pines.

To read Thoreau is almost to taste this elixir, and, with the unbearably tactile sense he gives us of its absence, to crave it all the more.

3

The Little Woman
Who Started the Great War

Speaking from the sickbed to which he has been consigned since he was shot in the spine in 1972, George Wallace made a public statement on the subject of what might be called comparative racism, North and South. *"The New York Times,"* he said (with, one imagines, a ghoulish grin, since he was talking to a *Times* reporter), "never did understand that segregation wasn't about hate. . . . I didn't hate anybody. I don't hate the man who shot me. When I was young, I used to swim and play with blacks all the time. You find more hate in New York, Chicago, and Washington, D.C., than in all the Southern states put together."

It is hard to know what to make of this claim. A reliable technique for measuring hatred has not, as far as I know, been invented; and no one (probably including Wallace himself) can say with certainty if the old segregationist, when he looks back and declares that "segregation was wrong," is still working at rehabilitating his reputation or, facing death, speaks from the heart. But ingenuous or not, his claim that the racial organization of the South was never built on hate is not a novel idea. It comes out of a long apologetic tradition through which Southerners have defended their version of apartheid and, before it, slavery itself, on the grounds that race relations in their quasi-feudal region have always been more stable and humane than in the brutal market culture of the North.

This idea goes back far in American history. It first became explicit about 150 years ago, when the sectional debate over race, which had been repeatedly restrained from breaking out into violence, turned urgent in the wake of the Mexican War. As western expansion accelerated, the question of whether and where slavery would be permitted in the new territories was renewed. It was a question on which the founding fathers had been evasive and euphemistic, and after the Missouri Compromise of 1820, it was, in effect, tabled. Throughout the 1840s, even as the abolitionist drumbeat began to rise, most Americans seem to have persuaded themselves that their nation could remain indefinitely divided along the geographical boundary (the famous 36° 30' parallel) which the Missouri Compromise had established.

In the 1850s, under pressure of new exigencies (the prohibition of slavery in California and the end of the slave trade in the District of Columbia were balanced by deferring the slavery question in the New Mexico territory and by enforcing the fugitive slave laws), the old political bargains began to come apart. Even if one reaches the judgment, as some historians have, that the decisive political questions raised by slavery were economic and, eventually, military, there now resumed a high-pitched debate about whether slavery could be justified anywhere on moral grounds.

To deal with this question, each side deployed what it understood to be the salient facts about slavery: the content of a slave's diet, housing conditions, access to medicine, state of religion, and so on. Reviewing these "facts," some Southerners actually came to believe that "the Negro slaves of the South are the happiest, and, in some sense, the freest people in the world." (Such arguments always entailed a favorable contrast to the "laboring masses" of the North, who lived in conditions "already intolerable [and] daily becoming worse.") Antislavery Northerners (such as the New York lawyer and philanthropist George Templeton Strong) replied that slavery "is the greatest crime on the largest scale known in modern history; taking into account the time it has occupied, the territory it covers, the number of its subjects, and the civilization of the criminals."

The slavery debate reached an impasse. One side presented the slaves as well clothed and well tended; the other found them barefoot and blistered in the sun. Each side came up with a different inventory of entities, such as shoes and overalls and quantities of meat and life expectancy. (This sort of statistical dispute continued long after emancipation, and eventually it became a retrospective argument among historians.) But the two sides never truly confronted the question of what these contested facts might mean. If, for instance, a slave did not show the scars of a leather strap on his back, what did this signify? Did it mean that he was happy on the job, or that his master was lenient, or that he was wily and elusive when committing infractions, or, perhaps, that he had all along been paddled instead of whipped so that when the time came to put him up for auction, he would not bear the marks of recalcitrance that might lower his fetching price?

As the answers to these sorts of questions became less and less reconcilable, they were more and more received by each side as calumnies from the other. It became a dispute about the merits of the contestants rather than about the welfare of the contested, like the proverbial squabble between medical experts (Melville devoted a chapter of *White-Jacket* to such a scene) who debate the relative merits of their surgical techniques while the patient, unnoticed, dies on the operating table.

On those occasions when the words of the victims were invoked (the 1840s and 1850s saw the publication of a growing number of narratives by slaves who had fled to freedom), the other side replied that such stories were fictions cobbled together by abolitionist editors from the ravings of illiterate blacks. To every claim there was a counterclaim. If Frederick Douglass reported in 1845 that he had seen slave women beaten with "heavy cowskin" until the "warm, red blood came dripping to the floor," five years later, in a passage about flogging in the navy, Melville would report (in an agnostic tone) that "the chivalric Virginian, John Randolph," had claimed to have witnessed aboard ship "more flogging than had taken place on his own plantation of five hundred African slaves in ten years." Such discrepant visions of the world of slavery were not only common but comprehensive. For every lynching in the South, Southerners pointed to a race riot in the North.

A few public figures did try to cut through the cant, as when Lincoln (in response to the incessant chatter about whether slavery was a good or bad thing for the enslaved) remarked that "people of any color seldom run unless there is something to run from." Lincoln understood that a human being's condition cannot be assessed like a plant's, by measuring the amount of nutrient it absorbs, or by comparing the damage it sustains outdoors from the sun with, say, the effects of indoor work near a blast furnace or a kiln. He knew that the basic point about slavery was being evaded, the fact (again in the words of George Templeton Strong) that it was nothing more or less than deliberate legislation intended to extinguish and annihilate the moral being of men for profit; systematic murder, not of the physical, but of the moral and intellectual being; blasphemy, not in word, but in systematic action against the Spirit of God which dwells in the souls of men to elevate, purify, and ennoble them.

With more authority than any white commentator could muster, Frederick Douglass agreed: "To make a contented slave, it is necessary to make a thoughtless one."

Douglass meant the word "thoughtless" not in the colloquial modern sense of inconsiderate or selfish but in the more precise, older sense of "without a thought." He knew that only by extinguishing the self-consciousness of the slave could the cotton kingdom truly be secure, which is why his owners were incensed when Douglass taught himself to read. "The graveyard of the mind" was one fugitive's phrase for his former life of servitude, and it is among the shameful facts of American history that so many whites accepted this work of soul-killing as necessary and defensible. To read our antebellum literature is to be appalled by how many leading American writers managed to blot out of their own awareness the possibility that slaves were not mentally vacant, that they had minds, that they were more than usable bodies.

Suppression of this basic human truth within the white mind is, finally, the only explanation for how John C. Calhoun, for instance, arguably the preeminent intellectual in American public life between the Revolution and the Civil War, could write in the late 1840s that "power can only be resisted by power" even as he rejected the right of black people to rebel against those who had subjugated them for two hundred years. More than a half-century earlier, Thomas Jefferson had declared that "those who labour in the earth are the chosen people of God," without recognizing that his words did honor to the black field hands who planted and pruned his gardens at Monticello while he wrote in his study about the rights of man.

There is only one way to understand this kind of moral obtuseness in people of otherwise exquisite intelligence. For most whites, black people not only were mysterious or alien or, as we say nowadays, "other," but, the fact is, did not exist at all.

The person who changed this situation was Harriet Beecher Stowe. The extraordinary book she wrote, which was published in 1852, *Uncle Tom's Cabin, or Life among the Lowly*, was not the first American work of imaginative writing that tried to get inside the experience of slavery. It was preceded by such abolitionist romances as Richard Hildreth's *The Slave; or, Memoirs of Archy Moore* (1836) and drew heavily on such tracts as Theodore Dwight Weld's *American Slavery as It Is* (1839). But it was the first book about slavery that touched the national nerve. Selling 10,000 copies in its first week and 300,000 within the first year, *Uncle Tom's Cabin* was denounced in the South as a "criminal prostitution of the high functions of the imagination to the pernicious intrigues of sectional animosity." As for its reception in the North, there is a story—probably apocryphal, but true to Stowe's spirit and intent—that President Lincoln greeted Stowe sometime in the early 1860s as "the little woman who wrote the book that started this great war."

Stowe's fame (and notoriety) followed years in which she had struggled to find her place in a family of arduous do-gooders, where she had long been assigned the place of meek little sister, especially to her older sister Catharine and her ambitious brothers Edward and Henry Ward. The mother of these (and five other) children, Roxana Foote Beecher, died when Harriet was barely five, and was remembered in the family as a woman of saintly patience and tenderness. Roxana left behind an image of maternal perfection that haunted Harriet as she tried, sometimes morbidly, to emulate it: "I don't know," she wrote to Catharine in 1826 at the age of fifteen, "as I am fit for anything, and I have thought that I could wish to die young, and let the remembrance of me and my faults perish in the grave, rather than live, as I fear I do, a trouble to everyone."

Harriet's father was the formidable Lyman Beecher, a thundering preacher apparently unafflicted with such doubts. Having remarried about a year after Roxana's death, he eventually added four children to the nine (one daughter had died in infancy) whom Roxana had borne. In 1826 he moved the family from Connecticut's Litchfield County to Boston, where he intended to vanquish the puny Unitarians who, he thought, were undermining the old Puritan stronghold. In 1832, eager for a bigger campaign, he moved on to Cincinnati in order to lead the fight to save the West from "Catholics and infidels." This southern Ohio town, in which Harriet grew to womanhood, married, and became a writer, was a raw, pork-packing city that ran on immigrant labor. Sanitation was mainly provided by pigs that ate up the citizens' garbage, converting it, in due time, into excrement that mixed with the stagnant water in the streets and dried into foul-smelling mud.

Undiscouraged by this city without proper churches or drains, Lyman Beecher was a tireless preacher who sermonized at home as much as in the meetinghouse. Harriet, as her most recent biographer, Joan Hedrick, says in one of many nicely precise phrases, was "positioned . . . to overhear what she needed to learn" from him, as well as from Catharine, in whose school at Hartford she had been both educated and apprenticed. All the Beechers were devoted to the imperatives of sacrifice and virtue, lessons Harriet absorbed so well that she wrote to a school friend that "self-denial . . . comes [to me] in the form of *pleasure*." The following year, at the age of seventeen, she wrote to one of her brothers that she

> was made for a preacher—indeed I can scarcely keep my letters from turning into sermons. . . . Indeed in a certain sense it is as much my vocation to preach on paper as it is that of my brothers to preach viva voce—I write note after note every day full of good advice & am used to saying "but you must consider" & "I wish you to remember"—& "think my dear" &c &c that you need not wonder to find me exhorting you.

If Harriet developed her preacherly instincts early, there was nothing to indicate that her particular target for amelioration would be the lives of black people. She "sometimes talks quite *Abolitiony* at me," wrote Catharine in the 1830s, "& I suppose quite Anti to the other side." It was only slowly that Harriet's imagination began to fix upon the outrage of slavery.

The issue first made itself directly felt in the life of the family when a series of debates over slavery broke out in the mid-1830s among students at Lane Theological Seminary, of which Lyman Beecher was president. By the time the commotion subsided, a substantial number of Lane's most committed students (including Theodore Weld) had stormed out in response to the trustees' decision to forbid student-led meetings, and to ban the antislavery societies that had been launched at the students' initiative. Half disciplinarian, half firebrand, Beecher had tried to maintain a middling position, but now he could only watch as much of his flock defected to Oberlin, where, under his evangelical rival Charles Grandison Finney, they would establish a long-standing tradition of racial and social progressivism.

A few years before, Harriet had married Calvin Stowe, a biblical scholar at Lane who regarded "Ultra Abolitionism [as] . . . *nasty Radicalism*," and from whose opinions—expressed no less authoritatively than were her father's—she now took her lead. Eventually, when her husband took up a position at Bowdoin, she would accompany him back East, and write *Uncle Tom's Cabin* in her native New England. But her intellectually formative years were spent with him in Cincinnati, just a few miles from a slave state; and it was here, in the contested Midwest, that Stowe became embroiled in the issues of the day. When an organizer of the Female Anti-Slavery Society called upon the younger Beecher ladies in the late 1830s, Harriet found the visitor's ideas, in Hedrick's words, "as 'ultra' as anything she had seen." But though she preferred something "intermediate," there were signs of a new restlessness in her spirit:

> Pray what is there in Cincinnati to satisfy one whose mind is awakened on this subject? No one can have the system of slavery brought before him without an irrepressible desire to *do* something, and what is there to be done?

It took nearly fifteen years for Harriet Beecher Stowe to answer this question. These were years during which her domestic responsibilities grew as she bore children of her own, while at the same time she achieved professional recognition as a writer of fictional sketches—first shared with friends, then published in women's magazines, until, in 1843, *Harper's* brought out her first book, *The Mayflower; or, Sketches of Scenes and Characters among the Descendants of the Pilgrims*. Although her brother Edward had by now emerged as a publicly committed abolitionist, the race issue remained abstract for most of the family, including Harriet. She had traveled to the South only once—a brief visit to a Kentucky plantation when she was in her early twenties—and there is some evidence that in 1839 she hired a black serving girl, probably a slave from across the river contracted out by her master, who collected most of her wages. Some of the stories Stowe wrote around this time were little more than jokes at the expense of "stupid . . . staring" housemaids whose incompetence at making beds was a vexation for the mistress of the house.

How did this woman, first contending with her taxing family, then caught in the swirl of public events, develop the fervor and courage to produce one of the most incendiary books on the subject of race ever to be composed in this country? The beginnings of an answer must be sought in Stowe's experience as a woman. Like many mothers in her time, Harriet Beecher Stowe had to bear the unbearable experience of losing a child. It happened to her three times—the death by cholera of her eighteen-month-old baby Charley in 1849; again, ten years later, when her son Henry drowned while a student at Dartmouth; and, much later, as a woman in her seventies, when she kept a deathbed vigil beside her invalid daughter Georgianna. One way that she dealt with the first stunning tragedy was to transform it into the fictional death of Eva St. Clare in *Uncle Tom's Cabin*, the angelic girl who befriends her parents' house slave, Tom, and recites Revelation with him, certain that they will live forever as equals in the kingdom of God. Eva's death has become (along with Little Nell's in Dickens's *The Old Curiosity Shop*) the most famous child death in nineteenth-century fiction—a "lingering and sainted death," as Ann Douglas has described it, which invites us "to bestow on her that fondness we reserve for the contemplation of our own softer emotions." Stowe was certainly a writer who allowed her readers to bathe in the sweetness of their own compassion.

But touching her readers with sentiment was only a part of the accomplishment of *Uncle Tom's Cabin*, and it was the lesser part. Stowe's breakthrough was that she enlarged the scope of sentiment so that black people, previously kept outside of its range, were suddenly awash in it. For this purpose, too, she had precursors, writers like John Pendleton Kennedy, who, in his book of plantation sketches, *Swallow Barn* (1832), had established the convention (which would culminate in *Gone with the Wind*) of portraying whites and blacks living together in fond mutual service. But into this picture Stowe introduced a range of extreme situations that had been previously banned from the genre, situations calculated to stir her readers' sympathy and admiration for the plight and resolve of the slaves, whom she thereby rendered more human than they had ever appeared before.

Early in the book, for instance, we witness the flight of the slave Eliza, whose "maternal love [is] wrought into a paroxysm of frenzy" when she learns that her master, under financial duress, has decided to sell her child. Uncle Tom, who is to be sold as well, resolves to accept his fate, but declares that it " 'tan't in *natur* for [Eliza] to stay," and endorses her shocking plan to escape with her child. Then, in a chapter that became a favorite subject for illustrators and was often adapted for the stage, Eliza bolts for freedom with her child in her arms, bounding, in the climactic scene, from the Kentucky shore across shards of ice in the Ohio River to the free state on the other side.

Later, in a book that is organized through a series of symmetries—the force of the market vs. the power of love, male calculation vs. female sensibility—we witness the terrible fate of the man who had stayed behind. The last chapters are devoted, in relentless detail, to the beatings endured by Tom as he is dragged deeper and deeper into the swampish hell of Simon Legree's plantation. When tempted by a fellow slave to kill his tormentor, Tom replies:

> No, ye poor, lost soul, that ye mustn't do. The dear, blessed Lord never shed no blood but his own, and that he poured out for us when we was enemies. Lord, help us to follow his steps, and love our enemies.

Both these instances of conquest over suffering—Eliza prevails in this life, Tom becomes a martyr—are written out as unabashed melodrama. They are shrieks more than arguments. It has been said that *Uncle Tom's Cabin* was written in tears rather than in ink. It was a book composed in the same frame of mind in which Stowe, a few years earlier, had conveyed to her absent husband the news that their son had died of cholera:

> I have just seen him in his death agony, looked on his imploring face when I could not help nor soothe nor do one thing, not one, to mitigate his cruel suffering, do nothing but pray in my anguish that he might die soon.

This image of the child beyond help of his mother's love is the source and inspiration of Stowe's creative power. "The distance," Joan Hedrick writes, "between this 'special child' enshrined in nineteenth-century literature and daguerreotypes and the slave child removed from parents as soon as profitable was as vast as it was unremarked upon." The key to Stowe's achievement was that she not only remarked upon this distance, but, by creating *Uncle Tom's Cabin* out of her own most private grief and outrage, began the process of closing it.

Stowe had a virtually religious commitment to the sanctity of domestic life. She did occasionally give vent to outbursts of disgust at what she called, in an almost reproachful letter to her husband, the "dark side of domestic life":

> It is a dark, sloppy, rainy, muddy, disagreeable day, and I have been working hard (for me) all day in the kitchen. . . . I am sick of the smell of sour milk, and sour meat, and sour everything, and then the clothes *will* not dry, and no wet thing does, and everything smells mouldy; and altogether I feel as if I never wanted to eat again.

But she always continued to believe, as she wrote in the mid-1860s, that "even the small, frittering cares of women's life—the attention to buttons, trimmings, thread, and sewing-silk—may be an expression of their patriotism and their religion." Stowe complained about the decadent women of modern times who hire "operators [to] stretch and exercise their inactive muscles," and she celebrated women of old who had "knowledge of all sorts of medicines, gargles, and alleviatives . . . [and] perfect familiarity with every canon and law of good nursing and tending." Indeed, "to be really great in little things, to be truly noble and heroic in the insipid details of every-day life, is a virtue so rare as to be worthy of canonization."

These are not the words of one who would fundamentally revise the way in which women understood their place in the world. With respect to the traditional family, Stowe was no reformer; she was a passionate conservative. *Uncle Tom's Cabin* is a study in how white and black families are deformed by slavery, how black women are degraded into prostitution, and white women, instinctually warm, turn cold. If it is a book particularly for and about women, it has a recuperative aim rather than a revolutionary one. It celebrates motherhood as the center of all domestic tranquillity, familial and national. It is a paean to the child-nourishing woman, as expressed in the miraculous triumph of Eliza's superhuman strength on behalf of her child, or in the memory that haunts Legree of his own mother, whom he had once spurned but for whom he longs as the one power that can still save him from damnation.

In fact, even as she grew up amid the anti-Catholic tirades of her father, Stowe seems to have had a sneaking sympathy for the Roman religion, which places the image of the Madonna at the center of devotion. *"Uncle Tom's Cabin,"* as Hedrick writes, "was the Protestant equivalent of the Roman Catholic mass, a dramatic re-enactment of the Crucifixion" in which Tom's body is the focus of the sacrament. To this point, one might add that *Uncle Tom's Cabin* is also an extended *pietà*, Stowe's meditation on the loss of a beloved child. In developing this Madonna theme, Stowe was enlarging upon what had become a convention of the slave narratives, as here expressed a few years earlier by Douglass:

I never saw my mother, to know her as such, more than four or five times in my life; and each of these times was very short in duration, and at night. She was hired by a Mr. Stewart, who lived about twelve miles from my home. She made her journeys to see me in the night, travelling the whole distance on foot, after the performance of her day's work. She was a field hand, and a whipping is the penalty of not being in the field at sunrise . . . I do not recollect ever seeing my mother by the light of day. She was with me in the night. She would lie down with me, and get me to sleep, but long before I waked she was gone. . . . She died when I was about seven years old, on one of my master's farms, near Lee's Mill. I was not allowed to be present during her illness, at her death, or burial. She was gone long before I knew any thing about it. Never having enjoyed, to any considerable extent, her soothing presence, her tender and watchful care, I received the tidings of her death with much the same emotions I should have probably felt at the death of a stranger.

The very power of this writing belies the assertion of emotional numbness that it reports. But as a piece of rhetoric it effectively dramatizes the fact that inspired Stowe's own critique of the "peculiar institution": that slaves were subject to an emotional deprivation which every mother of the time either felt or feared— the forcible separation of mother from child. When a child died of cholera, there was nothing to be done. But when a whole race of mothers and children was rent apart by a human institution, there was something one could do.

★　　★　　★

Uncle Tom's Cabin was Stowe's effort to save the black family. It was a major event in our history because, as Hedrick says, Stowe's "political achievement was to make a national audience see the subjectivity of black people," even if "what she herself saw was filtered through a white woman's consciousness." Recently, Philip Fisher, a tough-minded critic not notably drawn to the literature of sentimentality, has gone so far as to call it one of those rare books that actually "install new habits of moral perception" in our culture, in this case the new habit among whites of believing the proposition (preposterous before Stowe wrote, self-evident after) that "a black is a person."

This achievement merits our grateful amazement. Stowe "told the story" of the slaves, as the black poet Paul Laurence Dunbar put it, and "the whole world wept / At wrongs and cruelties it had not known." Yet it must also be acknowledged that her "white woman's consciousness" was a limiting one. As James Baldwin charged in a furious essay fifty years ago, she could not stop "evading [the] complexity" of her subject. If her maternal compassion had for the first time transformed slaves from an abstraction into human beings, it rendered them as no more than children. And when she wrote about black people safely removed from the depravities of the South, she reverted to convention and caricature. Nearly two decades later, in *Oldtown Folks* (1869), a book largely based on her husband's reminiscences of his boyhood in Natick, Massachusetts, she writes of blacks as a "tribe of little darkies" for whom "a side gallery" in the meetinghouse is appropriated. Among them are "fat, roly-poly" Jinny, and "jolly old Caesar," who can "gobble like a turkey so perfectly as to deceive the most experienced old boggler on the farm . . . and was *au fait* in all manner of jigs and hornpipes." These blacks are not people; they are mascots for the amusement of white folks.

Stowe's passion on the subject of race was a form of what Emerson, speaking of the abolitionists, had called "love afar." Like many of her contemporaries, she was drawn to the idea of African repatriation for emancipated slaves: "Let the church of the North receive these poor sufferers," she wrote at the conclusion of *Uncle Tom's Cabin*, ". . . until they have attained to somewhat of a moral and intellectual maturity, and then assist them in their passage to those shores [Liberia] where they may put in practice the lessons they have learned in America." Behind this hope there lies the fear that Baldwin hinted at when he remarked that "the wet eyes of the sentimentalist betray [an] aversion to experience, [a] fear of life." If the "perfectly submissive" Tom stands at the center of *Uncle Tom's Cabin*, he is surrounded by angry slaves, personifications of black rage, of whom one of the slave owners says, "Our system is educating them in barbarism and brutality. We are breaking all humanizing ties, and making them brute beasts; and if they get the upper hand, such we shall find them."

In the end, Harriet Beecher Stowe looked on the phenomenon of slavery through the clean moral categories of the Yankee reformer, and what she saw was a race of children being abused by a race of fiends. She could not grasp the strange mutual dependence of blacks and whites in the South—their perverse intimacy. This is where George Wallace's point about hatred in the North outrunning that of the South is not entirely dismissible. Stowe sensed the force of the point when she reveals that Legree himself is a displaced New Englander, and when she invents the character of an indignant Vermont spinster, an "absolute bond-slave of the '*ought*' " who comes South wanting "to be kind to everybody" but finds that it "fairly turned her stomach" to see blacks and whites touching one another. "As to kissing," that is simply beyond her imagination. Although the character of Miss Ophelia is an indictment of the fastidious New England temperament, it is also, in some measure, a self-portrait.

Uncle Tom's Cabin is a book that exemplifies the distance between righteous antagonism to evil institutions and awareness of the full humanity of the victims. To sweep away the oppressive structures is to take only a first step toward recognizing, in Baldwin's words, that no person, black or white, is "merely a member of a Society or a Group." It is a strange experience to read *Uncle Tom's Cabin* in our age of multiculturalism, when calls abound to free ourselves from the shibboleth of individualism in order to discover which ethnicity or tribe or interest group gives us our true identity. To read Stowe in this atmosphere is to be reminded of how immensely difficult it is—for the paternalistic liberal as well as for the candid racist—to see beyond the colors and categories, and to pay genuine respect to what Baldwin called the "resolutely indefinable" human being within.

★ 4 ★

The Two Lincolns

When the Republican Party chose him in May 1860 to run for President, Abraham Lincoln started to see double:

> A very singular occurrence took place the day I was nominated at Chicago four years ago, of which I am reminded tonight. In the afternoon of the day, returning home from downtown, I went upstairs to Mrs. Lincoln's sitting room. Feeling somewhat tired, I lay down upon a couch in the room, directly opposite a bureau upon which was a looking glass. As I reclined, my eye fell upon the glass, and I saw distinctly *two* images of myself, exactly alike, except that one was a little paler than the other. I arose and lay down again, with the same result. It made me quite uncomfortable for a few moments, but some friends coming in, the matter passed out of my mind.

As the United States was splitting into two, Lincoln felt something similar happening to him, or so it would seem, if we can trust these eerie words, reported in 1865 by the portrait painter Francis Carpenter. Lincoln may even have had a presentiment that a spectral twin would accompany him through life and beyond. Already before the start of his presidency, he was participating in the construction of his own myth with carefully posed photographs, with the few personal words he wrote or spoke in public, and even with his choice of confidants. After his death, the process of mythologizing continued: he was swiftly memorialized as a giant of ages past, and each successive future age has reconceived him in relation to its own preoccupations.

The ceaseless work of reckoning anew with Lincoln depends in part on what David Donald, his most recent biographer, calls "conversations recorded by reliable witnesses." For this reason, everyone interested in Lincoln has to decide sooner or later whom to trust. Was Billy Herndon—Lincoln's law partner, who blamed Mary Todd for his friend's fatigue and distraction—a "reliable witness"? What about Frederick Douglass, who reported that in their last interview Lincoln remarked, "I hate slavery as much as you do"? The eminent scholar Don E. Fehrenbacher, in collaboration with his wife, Virginia, has collected the raw material of Lincoln lore and sorted it by degrees of credibility. In their fascinating book, *Recollected Words of Abraham Lincoln*, we have the source of the legend that Lincoln wrote the Gettysburg Address on an envelope just before delivering it (Andrew Curtin, governor of Pennsylvania) and of the tradition (invented by Lincoln's Illinois friend Isaac Cogdal and publicized by Herndon) that the death of his beloved Ann Rutledge left him near despair, unable to bear the thought of rain falling on her grave.

Each attributed remark is graded by the Fehrenbachers according to a scale of A (for entries most likely to be authentic) through E (for those that ought to be removed from the Lincoln gospel and treated as apocrypha). It seems rude to be less than grateful for the Fehrenbachers' painstaking labor, but I find myself sorry to learn that Lincoln might not have said about a vain politician that if he "had known how big a funeral he would have had, he would have died years ago." They give this remark a C; I'd give it an A+. I'd like to believe (as reported by the owner of the Springfield drugstore where Lincoln was a customer in the 1850s) that when asked what was the matter with Willie and Tad as they screamed in tandem, Lincoln replied, "Just what's the matter with the whole world. I've got three walnuts and each of them wants two." And alas, it turns out that he also might not have said, in countenancing interracial marriage, that "if a white man wants to marry a Negro woman, let him do it—if the Negro woman can stand it."

This book is not reassuring about the possibility of writing "true" history. But does it really matter? In fact, as the Fehrenbachers acknowledge, "the legendary Lincoln, created in part out of dubious recollective material, may have been, in the long run, as powerful an influence in American life as the historical Lincoln." They have given us a glimpse not so much of the historical Lincoln as of the Lincoln created by the collective American imagination. If he did not exist, it would have been necessary to invent him.

In fact, it *was* necessary to invent him. Why is Lincoln the only American President regarded over many generations with something approaching religious devotion? There is a clue, I believe, in a phrase one shrewd contemporary used to describe him: he was "the pattern American," Nathaniel Hawthorne said. A mirror in which ordinary people saw themselves in all their defects and dignity, Lincoln always felt under hostile inspection by what his private secretary, John Hay, called the "patent-leather, kid-glove set." During the speech at Cooper Union that established him as a national candidate, he worried "before he became warmed up" that his suit showed "the creases made while packed in the valise" (according to Herndon). In the words of an Illinois friend, "he never felt his own utter unworthiness so much as when in the presence of a hotel clerk or waiter."

But Lincoln did not primp or posture in response to these anxieties; he was an iconoclast who never spared himself from his own leveling wit. According to one witness, he spoke of making his first trip to Massachusetts "with hayseed in my hair . . . to take a few lessons in deportment." This is the Lincoln of Herndon and Sandburg, whose un-Eastern folksiness was picked up by Will Rogers and Harry Truman, eventually to become a commodity sold to the public by Garrison Keillor and the like. Diagnosed with a mild form of smallpox, this Lincoln tells his physician, "There is one consolation about the matter, Doctor, it cannot in the least disfigure me." It would be difficult to find comparable remarks among the attributed (not to mention the documented) sayings of the bewigged and solemn Presidents who preceded him.

It was Lincoln who invented self-denigration as a political style. But how does this homely jokester of legend fit with the substantive Lincoln of record? For one thing, both have a taste for broad humor. "If it were not for these stories, jokes, jests," says Lincoln, according to Herndon, "I should die. They give vent—are the vents—of my moods and gloom." The historical Lincoln, explaining his retreat from an early courtship (in a letter whose authenticity seems secure), wrote that he realized his mistake when, looking upon the woman who once had pleased him, he found himself thinking instead of his "mother; and this, not from withered features, for her skin was too full of fat, to permit its contracting into wrinkles, but from her want of teeth, weatherbeaten appearance in general, and from a kind of notion that ran in my head, that *nothing* could have commenced at the size of infancy, and reached her present bulk in less than thirtyfive or forty years." In our antinormative age, jokes about body shape tend to be denounced as cruel, but for Lincoln the point was to acknowledge that most human beings are inelegant specimens (Herndon lovingly described his tall friend as so long-legged that when he sat, "a marble placed on his knee . . . would roll hipward, down an inclined plane"), and thereby to explode the pretension of being enchanted by oneself.

The prairie boy of legend and the Lincoln of record share more than wicked wit. They hate pomposity and are unfailingly alert to the stirrings of pride. The real Lincoln accrued enormous power while never presuming that the possession of power confers any special merit on its possessor. He referred bitterly to those occasions when he had to sign the execution orders of courts-martial as "butcher-days," and, though surrounded by flatterers and the trappings of high office, he never doubted that he was driven by forces larger than his own will. In a letter in 1864 to the Kentucky journalist Albert Hodges, he refused any "compliment to my own sagacity. I claim not to have controlled events, but confess plainly that events have controlled me." The Fehrenbachers' book is filled with echoes of this well-known remark, as when the ex-slave Sojourner Truth praised him for being the only President who had done anything for her people, to which Lincoln is said to have replied, "And the only one who had such opportunity. Had our friends in the south behaved themselves, I could have done nothing whatever."

A single, unbroken theme emerges from this book full of spurious stories, and it is perfectly continuous with the Lincoln who exists independent of it. This theme is his lifelong contempt for the idea that accidents of worldly rank imply a hierarchy of intrinsic worth. Variously expressed through humor, anger, piety, and self-doubt, this principle is what both the actual and legendary men were essentially about. From the actual Lincoln, one hears it at its purest in the short speech he delivered in February 1861 at Independence Hall in Philadelphia, where he had stopped en route to his inauguration. Amid rumors of an assassination plot (a few hours later he would switch secretly to a train at Baltimore, which then took him to Washington by night), he remarked, "I have never had a feeling politically that did not spring from the sentiments embodied in the Declaration of Independence." Then he elaborated:

> I have often pondered over the dangers which were incurred by the men who assembled here and adopted that Declaration of Independence. I have pondered over the toils that were endured by the officers and soldiers of the army, who achieved that Independence. [*Applause*] I have often inquired of myself, what great principle or idea it was that kept this Confederacy so long together.
>
> It was not the mere matter of the separation of the colonies from the motherland; but something in that Declaration giving liberty, not alone to the people of this country, but hope to the world for all future time. [*Great applause*] It was that which gave promise that in due time the weights should

be lifted from the shoulders of all men, and that *all* should have an equal chance. [*Cheers*] This is the sentiment embodied in that Declaration of Independence.

Now, my friends, can this country be saved upon that basis? If it can, I will consider myself one of the happiest men in the world if I can help to save it. If it can't be saved upon that principle, it will be truly awful. But, if this country cannot be saved without giving up that principle—I was about to say I would rather be assassinated on this spot than to surrender it.

Today it may seem callow to take very seriously this pledge of allegiance to equal opportunity as a universal principle. In 1861, however, neither Lincoln's Philadelphia audience nor the secessionists (who, in response to his election, had already moved to break up the Union) doubted that he meant exactly what he said. When he declared that "in due time," the weights should be lifted from the shoulders of all men, it was widely understood that "weights" meant slavery and that "due time" meant that slavery was doomed to die soon. As for the phrase "all men," it meant just that. All men. Black as well as white.

About a year earlier, in New Haven, speaking not far from the site of a shoe workers' strike, he had put the matter even more explicitly:

I am glad to see that a system of labor prevails in New England under which laborers *can* strike when they want to, where they are not obliged to work under all circumstances, and are not tied down and obliged to labor whether you pay them or not! I *like* the system which lets a man quit when he wants to, and wish it might prevail everywhere. One of the reasons why I am opposed to Slavery is just here . . . I want every man to have the chance—and I believe a black man is entitled to it—in which he *can* better his condition—when he may look forward and hope to be a hired laborer this year and the next, work for himself afterward, and finally to hire men to work for him!

Now that the "American dream" is more and more becoming a cruel deception, this statement may sound no different from that of a hack politician peddling the entrepreneurial myth. But when Lincoln said that black men should have the right to become employers, it was hardly something a politician could say casually, especially since he did not rule out the possibility that their employees might be white. And this at a time when no sitting President had ever gone on record to express personal opposition to slavery.

What was the source of Lincoln's antipathy to the "peculiar institution," and how deep did it run? Was he really offended, as he once claimed, by the sight of slaves on a canal boat "strung together precisely like so many fish upon a trot line"? The Fehrenbachers' book is not much help with these perennial questions precisely because it is authoritative about the dubious authority of its contents. Take, for instance, the problem of motive raised by a famous letter written in 1862 to Horace Greeley, in which Lincoln insisted that "my paramount object in this struggle *is* to save the Union, and is *not* either to save or to destroy slavery. If I could save the Union without freeing *any* slave I would do it, and if I could save it by freeing some and leaving others alone I would also do that." Doubtless authentic (they were written in

Lincoln's hand), these words come from the same man who a few years earlier had said, "I can not but hate" the "*declared* indifference" of Senator Douglas on the question of whether slavery should live or die.

These two public statements seem to' need mediation. One comes expectantly upon a comment from a reporter for the New York *Tribune*, Greeley's paper, that Lincoln had spelled out to a Chicago congressman exactly what he had meant: "The meaning of his letter to Mr. Greeley was this: that he was ready to declare emancipation when he was convinced that it could be made effective and that the people were with him." But the chain of transmission of this remark begins with the congressman, who tells it to the newspaperman, who tells it to an abolitionist activist, in whose papers it was ultimately found. Accordingly, the Fehrenbachers give it a flat D.

The problem is summed up in Lincoln's own words (as transcribed by the usually reliable John Hay): "It is impossible to determine the question of the motives that govern men or to gain absolute knowledge of their sympathies." Still, impossible as it may be, knowing how hot or cool were Lincoln's feelings about the suffering of the slaves has never been more important to his standing in the American pantheon than it is today. It is a question that cannot be begged. We can discount it as ahistorical; we can object to holding the past accountable to our own standards of enlightenment; we can even quote Lincoln quoting scripture: "Let us not judge that we be not judged." But the fact is, the persistence of our few national symbols depends on our ability to appropriate them for use—and there is reason to wonder whether Lincoln, the most durable of these symbols, is becoming another casualty of our race-obsessed age.

I believe that Lincoln spoke, and acted, out of profound revulsion at the outrage of slavery—something quite different from Jefferson's sporadic qualms and fears. But I state this conviction as a belief because it is no more or less demonstrable than any religious or aesthetic judgment. Here, from Lincoln's speech on the Dred Scott decision, is one of the key interpretable passages:

All the powers of the earth seem rapidly combining against [the Negro]. Mammon is after him; ambition follows, and philosophy follows, and the Theology of the day is fast joining the cry. They have him in his prison house; they have searched his person, and left no prying instrument with him. One after another they have closed the heavy iron doors upon him, and now they have him, as it were, bolted in with a lock of a hundred keys, which can never be unlocked without the concurrence of every key; the keys in the hands of a hundred different men, and they scattered to a hundred different and distant places; and they stand musing as to what invention, in all the dominions of mind and matter, can be produced to make the impossibility of his escape more complete than it is.

I cannot read this without hearing the theme of human equality surging in it. Therefore, I find it perfectly plausible that Lincoln might have called the Fugitive Slave Law of 1850 "ungodly" (the source is the abolitionist Alonzo Grover) or remarked (according to a New York businessman, James Gilmore) that "the war has educated the people into abolition."

And yet it is also true that the historical Lincoln, in his speech on the Dred Scott case, speaks of "a natural disgust in the minds of nearly all white people, to the idea of an indiscriminate amalgamation of the white and black races." Is this merely a description of a prevailing public attitude? (It takes a long search to find any mid-nineteenth-century spokesman who favored social equality between black and white.) Or is it an endorsement? At the end of this line of questions there is no consensus.

On the more dispassionate question of why Lincoln thought slavery intolerable in a society putatively based on individual rights, there is something closer to a certain answer. He clearly believed that the violation of rights for anyone threatens the rights of everyone. This view was summed up in the extraordinary fragment on slavery that he composed in a meditative moment, probably in 1854:

If A. can prove, however conclusively, that he may, of right enslave B.—why may not B. snatch the same argument, and prove equally, that he may enslave A.?—

You say A. is white, and B. is black. It is *color*, then; the lighter, having the right to enslave the darker? Take care. By this rule, you are to be slave to the first man you meet, with a fairer skin than your own.

You do not mean *color* exactly?— You mean the whites are *intellectually* the superiors of the blacks, and therefore have the right to enslave them? Take care again. By this rule, you are to be slave to the first man you meet, with an intellect superior to your own.

But, say you, it is a question of *interest*; and, if you can

make it your *interest*, you have the right to enslave another.
Very well. And if he can make it his interest, he has the right
to enslave you.

Here, in full view, is Lincoln's proto-modern conviction that the
very idea of race is incoherent. It is, as we would say today, "socially constructed"— a monstrous idea, liable to turn on the
masters who invented and relied on it. Its poison infiltrates everywhere and cannot be contained.

The only antidote to this poison is the idea of the individual,
and Lincoln returns again and again to this axiom of individual
rights. "A man who denies other men equality of rights is hardly
worthy of freedom," he says, in another comment recorded by
Hay, "but I would give even to him all the rights which I claim
for myself"; and the Fehrenbachers' book is peppered with versions of the argument that reclaiming these rights for black people
will serve the best interest of whites: "I do believe, that it will
result in good to the white race as well as to those who have been
made free by this act of emancipation."

There is in Lincoln a universalizing impulse (Herndon quotes
him extolling "universal education" and "the universal ballot")
that cuts across the flimsy barriers by which people try to wall
themselves off from those they deem unworthy of inclusion in
their circle. His mind was always moving away from the incidental
differences among people and toward the affinities and linkages
between them—sometimes to their credit (Herndon quotes him
on democracy: "the intelligence of the mass of our people was
the light and life of the republic") and sometimes to their shame
(on human motivation: "at bottom, the snaky tongue of selfishness
will wag out"). Lincoln recognized mankind and he recognized

persons; but he never recognized tribes or castes. And so he spoke fervently, in a documented speech in 1858, against the notion that the equality principle of the Declaration was somehow restricted to those descended by blood from its original beneficiaries, or to any other distinguishable group:

> We have besides these men—descended by blood from our ancestors—among us perhaps half our people who are not descendants at all from these men, they are men who have come from Europe—German, Irish, French and Scandinavian—men that have come from Europe themselves, or whose ancestors have come hither and settled here, finding themselves our equals in all things. If they look back through this history to trace their connection with those days by blood, they find they have none, they cannot carry themselves back into that glorious epoch and make themselves feel that they are part of us, but when they look through that old Declaration of Independence they find that those old men say that "We hold these truths to be self-evident, that all men are created equal," and they feel that that moral sentiment taught in that day evidences their relation to those men, that it is the father of all moral principle in them, and that they have a right to claim it as though they were blood of the blood, and flesh of the flesh of the men who wrote that Declaration [*loud and long continued applause*], and so they are.

Lincoln did not fail to recognize that this process—which, pejoratively, we call assimilation—entailed damage to the historical community of those "whose ancestors have come hither." Like Tocqueville, he recognized that "in democratic communities the imagination is compressed when men consider themselves"; but, again like Tocqueville, he also believed that "it expands indefinitely when they think of the state." Devotion to the state—to the Union—was his answer to the inescapable American problem of feeling unmoored from one's ancestral past.

Here we have the deepest reason why Lincoln's grip on our imagination may be weakening. In our time, the symbols through which he thought Americans could receive and transmit a sense of common destiny have been terribly vitiated. Consider this apposite comment from John Eaton, the army chaplain who became superintendent of freedmen under President Grant, who reported Lincoln's remark, at the height of the war, about

> people who thought the work on the Capitol ought to stop on account of the war, people who begrudged the expenditure, and the detention of the workmen from the army . . . [But] in his judgment, the finishing of the Capitol would be a symbol to the nation of the preservation of the Union. If [said he] people see the Capitol going on, it is a sign we intend the Union shall go on.

This is the Lincoln about whom Alexander Stephens, Vice President of the Confederacy, observed, "The Union with him in sentiment rose to the sublimity of a religious mysticism." In the age of Newt Gingrich, it takes a truly undiscourageable patriot to see the Capitol as a symbol of sublimity. Since Lincoln is finally the name we give to the beleaguered concept of individual rights under the protection of federal authority, his future as a national icon seems in doubt, especially now that his promise of upward mobility as a realistic hope for all Americans threatens to become a sham. And since the academic left has responded with little more than a mantra about group identity, it is increasingly difficult to invoke Lincoln as a precedent for serious thinking about the live problems of our day—income disparity, illegitimacy, affirmative action, abortion—problems that defy the old formula of individual rights on which Americans have traditionally found common ground.

Thus Lincoln the champion of self-reliance is in trouble for preaching an illusion. And Lincoln the antislavery man is in trouble for equivocating on racial equality. There are those who wish to explode the whole Lincoln "myth"—built in large part on hearsay and imperfect memory. But the demythologizers should think again. For, in their core convictions, the mythical figure and the actual man have been indistinguishable since even before his martyrdom, as one discerns in the words of Lincoln's greatest celebrant. During the winter of 1863–64, Walt Whitman spent his days tending Union wounded in hospitals in and around Washington, where the most he could do was offer a hand in comfort or write a letter home for a maimed or illiterate boy. Afterward, he would "wander about a good deal, sometimes at night under the moon," and on one mild February evening he stopped in front of the White House:

> The white portico—the palace-like, tall, round columns, spotless as snow—the walls also—the tender and soft moonlight, flooding the pale marble, and making peculiar faint languishing shades, not shadows—everywhere a soft transparent hazy, thin, blue moon-lace, hanging in the air—the brilliant and extra-plentiful clusters of gas, on and around the facade, column, portico, &c.—everything so white, so marbly

pure and dazzling yet soft—the White House of future poems, and of dreams and dramas, there in the soft and copious
moon . . .

After reading this beautiful meditation on Lincoln's as yet un-
realized dream, I find myself wondering how many more future
poems will be written.

5

Henry Adams and the End of the World

It is often said of the United States that it is a young country. As with any platitude, the force of this statement is weakened by its familiarity, but thinking about the span of certain American lives in relation to the age of the nation can help to restore our surprise at the truth of the claim. W. E. B. Du Bois was born during the administration of Andrew Johnson and died the year that John F. Kennedy died. Buckminster Fuller was a child when the battleship *Maine* was blown up in Havana harbor in 1898 and became a television "personality" during the Vietnam War. Speaking a few years ago at the centennial celebration of the birth of his father, Arthur Schlesinger, Jr., recalled a friend, James Rowe, who was Justice Holmes's last law clerk, to whom Holmes declared that "there is one thing I want you never to forget. You are speaking to a man who spoke to a veteran of the American Revolution." Schlesinger explained: "Holmes, born in 1841, must have talked as a child to someone who sixty years earlier had banged a drum in the Continental Army. The drummer boy, Oliver Wendell Holmes, Jim Rowe (who died only a year or two ago): there stands the history of the United States in three generations."

For Henry Adams, the history of the United States was in large part the history of his family. To encompass the period between the Revolution and World War I, the Adams family required not three generations but four. In his great memoir, *The Education of Henry Adams*, there is a moving account of John Quincy Adams (sixth President of the United States) walking his grandson, who had balked at going to school, "on a hot summer morning over a shadeless road" and planting him, "paralyzed by awe," in his schoolroom seat. "During their long walk he had said nothing; he had uttered no syllable of revolting cant about the duty of obedience and the wickedness of resistance to law; he had shown no concern in the matter; hardly even a consciousness of the boy's existence."

There is in this little parable a wistful remembrance not merely of his grandfather as the laconic Yankee but of a moment when the rules of civilization could be transmitted between the generations without having to be stated at all. For Henry Adams, who walked to school with the son of John Adams and who in his last years grew fond of young Eleanor Roosevelt, it was a gesture from the lost world into which he had been born: "Out of a medieval, primitive, crawling infant of 1838, to find oneself a howling, steaming, exploding, Marconing, radiumating, automobiling maniac of 1904 exceeds belief."

Even as Adams witnessed these staggering changes, from the silent rectitude of his grandfather to the brawling world of "goldbugs" (speculators) and slum bosses, he spent his life protesting against his exclusion from the scene of action. Watching from the sidelines as America entered the modern world, he was a young man at Lincoln's inaugural ball when Washington was little more than a swamp town with streets mostly of mud. Thirty years later, visiting the Chicago Exposition of 1893, he found the "very winds sarcastic and . . . sardonic" as they blew between the skyscrapers. Beginning in his youth, his own obsolescence was his favorite theme.

All his life he found a kind of comfort in proclaiming his infirmity. When his friend Clarence King was committed to the Bloomingdale insane asylum, Adams felt "a new bond of sympathy" between them, "he for having been in the asylum, and I for expecting to go there." When his older brother John died, Henry declared in a letter to an English friend that it was "something more than a loss. It is a notice to quit." Adams was always looking for portents of disaster and predicted, when it still required a lively imagination to conceive of carnage beyond the scale of a battlefield, that "someday science may have the existence of mankind in its power, and the human race commit suicide by blowing up the world."

Adams's life on the fringes of public affairs began in his early twenties when he went to England as private secretary to his father, Charles Francis Adams, whom Lincoln had appointed ambassador (and who was the last Adams to be widely discussed as a prospective President). While his contemporaries across the ocean were slaughtering each other in the first modern war, Henry passed his hours "in sleepy struggle with philosophers and political economists, varied occasionally with a walk, which ends sometimes in eating strawberries in Covent-Garden, or reading French newspapers at the Club." After the news reached London of the disaster at Bull Run, Henry wrote to his brother (who was serving in the Union Army), "I cannot stay here now to stand the taunts of everyone," but his parents easily dissuaded him from his intention to enlist.

After the war, and after he had achieved notice as a journalist, he was appointed to the editorship of the *North American Review* and made an assistant professor at Harvard. There he transformed the teaching of history by introducing seminars and a reserve system in the library, but he "detest[ed] large classes," and became "foul and abusive in my language to them, hoping to drive them away." Even as Adams complained of his oblivion, he remained a little churlish and frightened of the large audiences that wanted to hear him. He declined prizes for his great *History of the United States During the Administrations of Thomas Jefferson and James Madison* (1889–91), as well as honorary degrees, and in 1894 he sent his presidential address to the American Historical Association in the form of a letter from Mexico, where he was spending a well-timed vacation.

When Adams left Cambridge in 1877 ("the instruction of boys is mean work") and moved to Washington to observe the corruption scandals that had engulfed the Grant administration, he set up court as a kind of American Madame de Staël, and later built a house (designed by H. H. Richardson, with ornamented arches and a green onyx fireplace) across Lafayette Square, from which he could watch the White House. After Grant and Hayes were gone, his "pet aversion [became] Grover Cleveland, but he lives so near me that I can't throw a bomb at him without breaking my own windows." That was the way Adams liked it: being close enough to the center of power that action would be prohibitively costly to himself.

In later years Adams's friends called him "the old Cardinal" or "Porcupinus Poeticus," as his tone oscillated between a dignified jeremiad and a whine. Yet even in his self-indulgence as America's chief disfranchised intellectual—"I am torn between violent nausea of American politics, and strong desire to see the game played"—he spoke not solipsistically, but for a caste and generation whose grip on the country was being loosened, who feared, not without reason, for the nation's future. In 1865, when Lincoln was assassinated, Adams wrote to his brother in ingenuous fear: "The King being dead, what then? . . . Will the old set hold their ground, or is Seward and the long-lived race about him, to make way for a young America which we do not know?"

In the years that followed, Adams repeatedly answered his own question with tirades against the new business classes. Like many of his Progressive contemporaries, he regarded them as unwashed boors degrading the country. In his 1870 article on the effort by Jay Gould and James Fisk to corner the gold market (abetted, they thought, by Grant), Adams described Gould as having a "nature [that] suggested survival from the family of spiders: he spun webs, in corners and in the dark," and Fisk as "coarse, noisy, boastful, ignorant, the type of a young butcher." Later in life, Adams subsumed all such manipulators under the simple category "Jew." His anti-Semitism (which was, in Richard Hofstadter's phrase, "jocose and rather heavy-handed") made him suspicious of Dreyfus but did not extend to such connoisseurs of the threatened high culture as Bernard Berenson, to whom he wrote with courtly appreciation for sending him manuscripts of medieval music.

Adams's economic opinions were somewhat inconstant. Once he favored a controlled currency backed strictly by gold specie, but he was converted to bimetallism, which favored expansion of the currency supply by coining silver. He did this under the sway of his brother Brooks's theory that the greedy rich would always favor contraction of the money supply and thus incite social anarchy among the laboring poor, the result being a continual cycle of repression and social revolution. In the 1890s, when financial crisis triggered social unrest across the country, Adams was as disgusted with the radical labor leader Eugene Debs (he called him "Dictator Debs") as he was with Grover Cleveland's decision that "the government can safely use the army to shoot socialists." Such was the story of all Western history: stability was an elusive goal. (He considered the presidential campaigns of William Jennings Bryan, who ran on the populist platform of breaking the stranglehold of the corporations and banks, to be hopeless.) "As I am a constitutional pessimist," he wrote to John Hay in the 1890s, "and an anarchist by historical conviction, I see no way out of our mud-hole, and wait for you to bring me light and joy." This solicitation was made when Hay was already what Adams called a "valetudinarian."

The Adamses themselves were not immune to the booms and busts. Charles Francis, Jr., Henry's older brother, was president of the Union Pacific Railroad and was badly hurt by the Panic of 1893; and "my brother Brooks is always scared blue by the fear that the public will devour his last shilling and sit on him in the gutter." In the midst of the panic, Adams took note that gentlemen (in this case, a prominent shoe manufacturer who was a guest at the summer house of the Lodges) were beginning "daily [to] commit suicide off [the] rocks by walking into the water with their clothes and hats on." A conservative investor himself, Adams commented on this "usurer's world" with a Thoreauvian contempt: "I found Boston standing on its head, wild with terror, incapable of going to bed and brushing its weary old tusks in the morning; all this only because no one could get any money to meet his notes." At other times he sounds like a populist rabble-rouser (with the difference that his international perspective made London, rather than New York, the seat of satanic intrigue):

> The radical trouble is that man is by nature a liar. The London Times, in the thirty-eight years I have known it, has never once told the truth, unless it was on indifferent matters. The press is the hired agent of a monied system, and set up for no other purpose than to tell lies where its interests are involved. . . . The Church never was as rotten as the stock-exchange now is. . . . The trouble is that the whole thing pivots on London.

By the end of his life, Adams saw the United States overwhelmed by organized greed—and by the human fodder of that greed, the immigrant workers who drove down the price of labor, swelled the markets, and changed the cities beyond recognition. He heard these immigrants "snarling a weird Yiddish to the officers of customs," and, at the turn of the century, looking "out the club window on the turmoil of Fifth Avenue," he

> felt himself in Rome, under Diocletian, witnessing the anarchy, conscious of the compulsion, eager for the solution, but unable to conceive whence the next impulse was to come or how it was to act. The two-thousand-years failure of Christianity roared upward from Broadway, and no Constantine the Great was in sight.

This was Henry Adams as he is most often caricatured, and as he parodied himself: the New England kibitzer, the last of a beaten breed that would soon give way to a new group of intellectuals with different pedigrees (Herbert Croly, H. L. Mencken, Walter Lippmann) who were more attuned to the energies of the new age, for whom the New England heritage was merely one attenuated branch of the genteel tradition. This version of Adams was well represented a few years ago by Wallace Shawn in the television production of Gore Vidal's *Lincoln*—a slightly fey young cynic hanging back at the edges of the inaugural ball, curious about Lincoln because "if he should fail, there will no longer be a country. And since my family believes that we invented the whole thing, I'd certainly like to see what becomes of the remains."

It was as if Adams, thinking of himself as the weakened scion of a once robust New England family, were determined, before the fact, to fulfill his friend Henry James's prophecy that after "the subsidence of [the] great convulsion" of the Civil War, "the good American" (by which James meant someone with an absorptive consciousness like his own) "will be, without discredit to his well-known capacity for action, an observer." For Adams was always and everywhere the observer; and, in his remarkable letters, he wrote most of his observations down.

Sending home impressions from Tahiti, where he traveled in the early 1890s with the painter John La Farge, he "would be absolutely immersed in his letter-writing," even as an oiled young girl squatted on the mat beside him. Apparently celibate after the suicide of his wife (he was forty-seven when she died), he remarked on the unseemliness of late-life sexuality, and displayed an almost voyeuristic fervor in his unconsummated passion for

Elizabeth Cameron, the woman who became, in later years, a kind of madonna to whose sensibility he appealed for confirmation of his own. He reveled in his indignation and his discardedness as if he were a stranded time traveler: "When one cares for nothing in particular, life becomes almost entertaining. I feel as though I were at a theater—not a first class, but a New York theater." In the *Education* he refers to himself, always in the third person, as an eighteenth-century man and builds his narrative on the theme of his own anachronism. "Do you suppose," he wrote to an English friend in the 1860s, "that I had any news to tell you that was *not* about myself?"

Throughout the extraordinary letters, which fill more than 4,000 pages in six volumes superbly edited by a team of scholars including Adams's biographer, Ernest Samuels, we can follow Adams's education without what Lionel Trilling called "the excessive elaborations of irony" that characterize his late public writings. The whole life is here: the college boy's travels on the Continent; the bewildering years in London, when young Henry expected to find an antislavery nation of Wilberforces but discovered instead that the British government was cannily measuring the risk of cotton shortage against the prospect of an export market without tariffs. (Adams concluded that "it is never the hope of a future good . . . that actuates people.") In the 1870s he made himself a kind of public stenographer in Congress (as Samuel Johnson and Charles Dickens had done in Parliament) watching the legislators behave as paid agents of big business, and publishing their actions to the world. "For once," he felt, he had discovered a way to affect the national life while remaining the uncontaminated observer: "I have smashed things generally and really exercised a distinct influence on public opinion by acting on the limited number of cultivated minds."

The letters enable us to feel as well the strain of writing the *History*, a narrative of strife between Republicans and Federalists, written as if to recapitulate the late-life rapprochement between Jefferson and Adams's great-grandfather John, in which Thomas Jefferson is carried along against his instincts by the ineluctable growth of national power. During the years when Henry, with his wife, Clover, ran the liveliest salon in Washington, the letters were cheerful, bristling, and acerbic, and emerged almost daily. When, after her death, he stayed on as an owlish commentator on the political scene, he used his correspondence as a lifeline to his vanishing New England world.

If the private life, which is muted in the public writings, stands openly before us in the letters, so does the sheer power of Adams's mind as he applied it (after he ceased writing historical narrative) to the philosophy of history. In his *Letter to American Teachers of History*, he repeatedly invoked a dramatic fraction in which he found an analogue to the old Calvinist dogma of man's insignificance—that the earth (according to contemporary physicists) intercepts only $\frac{1}{2,300,000,000}$ of the total quantity of solar heat, the incalculably larger remainder being dissipated into the vacuum of space. The sun, Adams muses, "should be held to a sort of moral accountability because it utilizes" so little of its energy "on any known work, and degrades the rest indefinitely into space." In Adams's fascination with this Pascalian image of the prodigality of the cosmos, we arrive at the most characteristic exercise of his mind: the effort to find moral meaning in the bewildering phenomena that modern science was making visible to man.

★   ★   ★

A dams mused in the *Education* that "except as reflected in himself, man has no reason for assuming unity in the universe, or an ultimate substance, or a prime-motor. The a priori insistence on this unity ended by fatiguing the more active—or reactive—minds; and Lord Bacon tried to stop it. He urged society to lay aside the idea of evolving the universe from a thought, and to try evolving thought from the universe." The trouble was that although man had banished God (an alternative name for "ultimate substance" or "prime motor"), he had not—despite the Copernican revolution—truly convinced himself of his own marginality. His inductions about the workings of the universe were always obstructed by his sense of himself as telos, as, in the language of evolution, "the last term of a series beyond which . . . no further progress is materially possible."

What Adams saw, as he tried to grasp the implications of contemporary science, was that everything pointed away from this idea of man as the culmination of nature's purpose, and pointed instead to the truth of the second law of thermodynamics: that within closed systems energy tends constantly to dissipate as heat. That "the second law of thermodynamics rules biology with an authority fully as despotic as it asserts in physics" is confirmed for everyone by knowledge of one's imminent death. That the same law is ratified by history had not yet been systematically shown, Adams thought, but he was sure it was the instinct of every true historian to believe it.

Thus "the greatest historical work in the English language is called 'the Decline and Fall,' " and it was upon this work that Adams modeled his own *History*, in which he meditated (with explicit homage to Edward Gibbon) on the illusion of progress in the early American republic. There is even a way in which Adams seemed (long before he found his analogies in science) to conceive of American history as the dissemination of democratic energy to the world, with a consequent exhaustion at home: "when all the world stands on the American principle," he writes at the end of the Civil War, "where will be our old boasts unless we do something more." More broadly, when man "felt his own feebleness, and he sought for an ass or a camel, a bow or a sling, to widen his range of power, [it was] as he sought a fetish or a planet in the world beyond."

All of Adams's experience led him to feel that the spiral of history was downward. He filled his late essays with graphs and charts to illustrate this point. He read Max Nordau's *Degeneration* (1893) with approval and, I am sure, would have greeted Spengler's *Decline of the West* (1922) with assent. He had always been skeptical of the progressivist implications of evolutionary theory. Now he noted with satisfaction that "the Darwinist no longer talks of Evolution; he uses the word 'transformation,' " a much more neutral term for change:

In strictness, no doubt, water which falls and dynamite which expands, are equally degraded energies, but the mind is repelled by the figure of expansion. Because an energy is diffused like table-salt in water, it is not rendered less useful at all to an animal like man whose life is shut within narrow limits of intensity, who sends for a physician if his temperature rises a single degree, and who dies if it rises or falls 5° centigrade; whose bath must be tempered and his alcohol diluted; and whose highest ambition is to train and temper his own brute energies to obey law. Notoriously civilization and education enfeeble personal energy; *emollit mores*: they aim especially at extending the forces of society at cost of the intensity of individual forces. "Thou shalt not," is the beginning of law. The individual, like the crystal of salt, is absorbed in the solution, but the solution does work which the individual could not do.

This Emersonian passage is sanguine in its piety toward the transforming universal force that matches every loss with a proportional gain (Emerson called this the doctrine of "compensation"). But it is not Adams's final credo; it is a prologue to his belief that the new forces—the dynamo he saw at the Chicago Exposition in 1893, which "delighted me because it was just as chaotic as my own mind," and the X rays from the "supersensible" world of which he began to be aware after the Paris Exposition of 1900—are evidence of chaos within nature itself.

In his letter to the American Historical Association in 1894, Adams called for a science of history, but he warned that it would be resisted as a scandal by all the vested interests—by the church (with its commitment to the idea of providence); by the state (with its commitment to the "natural" rights of property); by the socialists (who held to the idea that history was evolving toward rationality). But the real scandal of Adams's "scientific history" was to consciousness itself: the idea that the little world of man was merely a short-lived offshoot of purposeless fire.

William James, among others, had little patience for Adams's apocalyptic gloom, and for his desire to extend the apparent laws of physics to the history, and destiny, of consciousness. In a trenchant letter to Adams, he wrote:

The *amount* of cosmic energy it costs to buy a certain distribution of fact which humanly we regard as precious, seems
to be an altogether secondary matter as regards the question
of history and progress. Certain arrangements of matter *on
the same energy level* are, from the point of view of man's
appreciation, superior, while others are inferior. Physically, a
dinosaur's brain may show as much intensity of energy-
exchange as a man's but it can do infinitely fewer things,
because as force of detent it can only unlock the dinosaur's
muscles, while the man's brain, by unlocking far feebler muscles, indirectly can by their means issue proclamations, write
books, describe Chartres Cathedral, etc., and guide the energies of the shrinking sun into channels which never would
have been entered otherwise—in short, *make* history.
Therefore the man's brain and muscles are, from the point
of view of the historian, the more important place of energy-
exchange, small as this may be when measured in absolute
physical units.

The "second law" is wholly irrelevant to "history"—save
that it sets a terminus—for history is the course of things
before that terminus, and all that the second law says is that,
whatever the history, it must invest itself between that initial
maximum and that terminal minimum of difference in energy
level.

And Henry James, too, in a beautiful letter written near the end
of both their lives, rebuked his old friend: "*Of course* we are lone
survivors, of course the past that was our lives is at the bottom of
an abyss—if the abyss *has* any bottom; of course, too, there's no
talking unless one particularly *wants* to. But . . . one *can*, strange

to say, still want to . . . You see I still, in presence of life (or of what you deny to be such), have reactions—as many as possible . . ."

These wonderfully sanative responses of the James brothers have the effect of making Adams seem a brooding misanthrope, but one should resist the indictment. In his own courageous way, Adams was driven by the peculiar spirit that has always both inspired and afflicted the greatest American writers: by an unembarrassed willingness to express the child's horror at the ubiquity of death, by the urge, as if in bedside prayer, to speak directly with God.

Within the ironically detached "Adams" of the *Education*, there is a fervent seeker: "to Adams the dynamo became a symbol of infinity . . . this huge wheel, revolving within arm's length at some vertiginous speed, and barely murmuring—scarcely humming an audible warning to stand a hair's breadth further for respect of power—while it would not wake the baby lying close against its frame." In this image of the immense power of the dynamo restrained by its own gentleness, or standing in Chartres Cathedral before the rose window of the Virgin "who shrank from the sight of pain," Adams was able to turn his revulsion at modernity into worship. "Unless you can go back to your dolls, you are out of place here," he reflected at Chartres, and he made, in his sixties, a reversion from the modern "feebleness of . . . fancy" to an aroused awareness of the divine.

Mont-Saint-Michel and Chartres was ostensibly a study of two great monuments of Romanesque and Gothic architecture, but it was really a marriage poem written by an old widower awaiting death. Adams's wife had killed herself in 1885 by swallowing the cyanide she used in her photographic darkroom. Now, years later at Chartres, "the quiet, restrained grace of the romanesque married to the graceful curves of and vaulting imagination of the gothic makes a union nearer the ideal than is often allowed in marriage." In this cathedral "the old romanesque leaps into the gothic under our eyes. . . . The two expressions are nowhere far apart; not further than the Mother from the Son. The new artist drops unwillingly the hand of his father or his grandfather; he looks back, from every corner of his own work, to see whether it goes with the old." But there are dissonances: the new tower at Chartres, "in comparison with the old, showed signs of a certain tendency toward a dim and distant vulgarity." And for this vulgarity Adams had a name: self-consciousness.

Here we arrive at the great paradox of Adams's lifework. He was, between Whitman and Mailer, the most self-conscious of our major writers, I think, defiantly asserting that by far the most interesting literary subject he could find was the action of his own mind. And yet it was precisely for his self-consciousness that he put himself on trial. It was his effort to escape himself that resulted in his greatest books, *Mont-Saint-Michel* and the *Education*, each written as if the garrulous writer of the letters had been refined by fire into a disembodied spirit.

If the irony of the late Adams is corrosive, it is meant to dissolve the self. There are hints of this procedure even in the early letters, as when he writes of a hike through the Scottish highlands, where his "shoes, crushing the wet sea-weed, called out at every movement bright, flashing phosphoric flames, so that we seemed to be walking on liquid fire." These walks through a prehuman landscape intimate that nature is not a park for man to play in, but an organism on whose outer skin man is either an eruption or a stray irritant. Later letters written on a trip to Japan, where he went under the tutelage of Ernest Fenollosa, pay uneasy tribute (no doubt an expression of what is nowadays called "Orientalism") to the unselfconscious quality of Japanese culture, where "the whole show is of the nursery," where, sleeping in an inn, Adams finds himself barely separated from his fellow guests by translucent screens and sliding doors, and where the children, women, and men all bathe together naked, unashamed.

Soon after Clover's suicide, we find Adams engaged in what Ernest Samuels calls the "macabre ritual" of reading the diaries of his youth and then burning them, volume by volume, in his onyx fireplace. Irony is the fire of the *Education*. It burns away the personal memories and leaves a floating consciousness trying to slip into phase with the flow of history. The surest sign that Adams wished to obliterate his own self-consciousness is that Clover's death is left entirely out of the *Education*. One feels that he speaks of it only by displacement, when writing of the horror of his sister's death by tetanus. He left it out, I suspect, because he could not bear to write about this event in the ironic voice of the rest of the "autobiography," as if it had happened at a distance, to be recorded by the bemused observer along with everything else.

The last letters, some dictated, others shortened by the loss of sight or hand control, are terribly moving. Calling himself "the venerable paralytic" or "the octogenarian rat," he writes to Henry James that "each day is an isolated fact, to be taken by itself and looked at as a dance." At Christmas 1914, he writes to Elizabeth Cameron as if time itself could be cut and pieced together into new patterns, and the divisions between words elided:

Yesterday my brother Charles sat an hour or two with me, and I think that, in fifty years more, I may be as young as he, but exactly how young it will be passes my figures. He is now just twentyseven when Lee surrendered. He thinks of Germans as rebels. I wish I did, but I am now in my Saint Augustincarnation, and see only the Civitas Dei. There are the Poinsettia and sunshines, if not much else, and we can't all be eighty years old.

After a series of strokes, he writes to Henry Cabot Lodge, who nearly fifty years earlier had been his favorite student, that "I can sit now for hours, quite still, with my hands before me, thinking of them, as all that is left worth a thought." It is as if he relinquishes his body and, by concentrating on losing his consciousness, saves himself: as Emerson put it and as Adams came, I think, to agree, "the discovery we have made that we exist . . . is called the Fall of Man."

6

The Short, Unhappy Life
of Stephen Crane

By the time he was twenty-five, Stephen Crane was famous, and before he reached thirty, he was dead. Born in New Jersey into a family that was, he said, full "of the old ambling-nag, saddle-bag, exhorting kind" of preachers, he died, probably of a mix of malaria and tuberculosis, in an English manor house to which he had moved with the madam of a Florida brothel. How he got from the pious household in Asbury Park to the fetid mansion in Sussex is a short but complicated story. It is, among other things, a preview of later American writers destroyed by early success. Moreover, Crane was aware of what was happening to him. "People may just as well discover now," he wrote in 1897, three years before his death, "that the high dramatic key of The Red Badge cannot be sustained." A little later he was complaining that "my importance has widened and everybody sits down and calmly waits to see me be a chump."

Crane sounds, in his frankest letters, like a typecast young actor searching for a new part: he had, all his life, preened and groomed himself for notice. His successes at military school were in marksmanship and baseball. At Syracuse University he was remembered as a fop who, in the cupola of his fraternity house, liked to smoke his hookah and hold forth on his exploits with gamblers and whores. On the evidence of his letters, it would seem that he never quite outgrew his adolescent self-consciousness. In 1892 the college boy writes consolingly to a prep school buddy in Virginia that if he should "lack females of the white persuasion" it was well to remember that "black is quite good—if—if its [sic] yellow and young." In 1896, the year of William Jennings Bryan's reform campaign for the presidency amid labor strife and deep social unrest, the world-famous novelist was using the phrase "social crisis" to refer to his anxiety about giving dinner-party toasts.

This was the writer whom Alfred Kazin had in mind when he said that Crane "cared not a jot which way the world went." He was a fin de siècle combination of two distinct but related literary types: the debunker (whom we recognize today in Tom Wolfe or Gore Vidal) and the "minimalist" (Frederick Barthelme or Mary Robison). Crane got his start writing newspaper dispatches from Jersey-shore hotels, in which the tourist attended posture classes to learn the "scientific" way of picking up a chair. He went on to Cuba and Greece as a war correspondent. Journalism was his schooling, and mockery the leading impulse of his early work, yet he did not exempt himself from the range of his contempt.

One of the bitterest passages in all his work, from a novel of 1899 called *Active Service*, tells of a reporter who convinces a bumpkin couple to allow a photograph to be taken of their deformed baby, who is expected to die momentarily:

Afterward as the correspondent and the photographer were climbing into their buggy, the mother crept furtively down to the gate and asked, in a foreigner's dialect, if they would send her a copy of the photograph. The correspondent, carelessly indulgent, promised it. [He] was elated; he told the photographer that the *Eclipse* would probably pay fifty dollars for the article and the photograph.

One can almost taste the nausea in this passage. There was a good deal of self-hatred in Stephen Crane.

While on a muckraking tour of Midwestern mining towns in 1894, Crane granted an interview to a young college journalist at the University of Nebraska named Willa Cather, who later recalled that "I have never known so bitter a heart in any man as he revealed to me that night." Crane was, as Cather sensed, something like a precocious George Sanders character, cackling at an early age over the absurd disproportion between the size of human emotion and the pettiness of the stakes. Much of his writing is committed to illustrating the absence, not just in art but in the affective life of human beings, of what T. S. Eliot was soon to call the "objective correlative" for emotion.

"The only way of expressing emotion in the form of art," Eliot decreed, "is by finding an 'objective correlative'; in other words, a set of objects, a situation, a chain of events which shall be the formula of that *particular* emotion; such that when the external facts, which must terminate in sensory experience, are given, the emotion is immediately evoked." According to Crane's parodic imagination, life itself was, in exactly these terms, an aesthetic botch: an incessant melodrama performed by overwrought actors whose "emotion" is always, in the phrase Eliot applied to the fretful Hamlet, "in excess of the facts as they appear"—excessive, that is, to everyone outside the affected self.

The reason for this seeming disproportion is that while there may be such entities as objective phenomena (bullets piercing human flesh in *The Red Badge of Courage*, injury by spilled acid in "The Monster," Crane's great story about a black man disfigured while rescuing a child from a laboratory fire), human feeling remains essentially private and incommunicable. Crane's world is thus populated by isolated perceivers, whose responses to phenomena (the sense of panic and pain in *The Red Badge of Courage*, the revulsion at the socially unassimilable freak in "The Monster") may sometimes converge, but who have no shared relation to anything that might be called stable truth. Thus *The Red Badge of Courage* is a book about a young man whose trivial head wound, incurred from a random rifle butt in the scramble of retreat, becomes, absurdly, a symbol of courage. It becomes such a symbol because it accidentally conforms, as one among many bloody gashes, to the visual grammar of war. But it signifies bravery in a world where bravery is a sham.

There is, still, an irresistible urge to read *The Red Badge of Courage* as a bildungsroman. It has long been an English teacher's favorite, because it has a conveniently interrogatory form: What, it obliges us to ask, does Henry Fleming learn? There are no civics-class answers to this question. If he learns anything, it seems to be that his mind makes the world, and that the world makes nonsense. At one point he walks, by what feels to him like a "religious half light," into a natural "chapel" formed by arching pine boughs. There he expects to find respite from the din of battle, but he discovers instead a green corpse with open mouth turned putrid yellow, along the upper lip of which runs a file of ants "trundling some sort of a bundle." The book is rich in colors; but the recurrent promise of green—to awaken and redeem—is

no more fulfilled than is the promise of red to humble the un-
scathed witnesses by confronting them with evidence of sacrifice.

On one occasion during Fleming's march, "the ranks opened
covertly to avoid [a] corpse. The invulnerable dead man forced a
way for himself. The youth looked keenly at the ashen face. The
wind raised the tawny beard. It moved as if a hand were stroking
it." Nature is jester here, providing simulacra of human desires
(in this case, a tender touch) but never the real thing. The reason,
Crane seems to be hinting, is that reality is only apprehensible
through the habitual or eccentric interpretations that the mind
projects onto raw phenomena. There is no neutral language for
the movement of the beard in the wind—unless it is the language
of aerodynamics or the physical properties of hair, which are, in
fact, the kind of empirical impasse toward which Crane's prose
was tending. Thus there is, for Crane, no intrinsic moral meaning
in the world. His biggest laugh is always at the expense of those
who think there might be one.

What is often missed in discussions of Crane is the degree to
which these habits of mind arose and found a responsive read-
ership in America in the aftermath of the Civil War. Barely ten
years after the publication of *The Red Badge of Courage*, William
James was putting quotation marks around "the true," and defin-
ing it as "only the expedient in the way of our thinking, just as
'the right' is only the expedient in the way of our behaving." This
was news in a culture saturated with religious certitude. Despite
Crane's relative philosophical (and even literary) innocence, *The
Red Badge of Courage* participates in this shift of epistemological
assumptions. It is a novel about a man whose inherited ideas of
truth fail him. Truth, as James described it, is "any idea that helps
us to *deal*, whether practically or intellectually, with either the

reality or its belongings, that doesn't entangle our progress in frustrations, that *fits*, in fact, and adapts our life to the reality's whole setting." Truth is a function of language, and a response to human need; but it is language that fails Henry Fleming as he gets entangled in the reality of war. His visions of chapels and valor and brawn cannot save him.

Like others who wrote and read about the war, Crane came to hate ornament. He stripped his prose virtually bare—yielding a style that, by the principle of contrast, makes the people in his fictions seem like compulsive prettifiers. Here is his slum girl in *Maggie: A Girl of the Streets*, contemplating the object of her passion:

> Maggie observed Pete. . . . His hair was curled down over his forehead in an oiled bang. His rather pugged nose seemed to revolt from contact with a bristling moustache of short, wire-like hairs. . . . His patent-leather shoes looked like murder-fitted weapons. . . . Maggie perceived that here was the beau ideal of a man.

Just as he treated Maggie with derision, Crane dismissed the popular novels of his day as "pink valentines." But in his compensatory "realism," he too often treated material that he did not really know. The characters in *Maggie*, for example, during their regular outbreaks of domestic violence, destroy the family furnishings again and again—a circumstance that led F. O. Matthiessen to remark that Crane was overlooking "a fact that Dreiser would not have forgotten, that there would have been no money to replace" the furniture after the first rampage. Matthiessen was right: Crane's real subject was not the texture, the lived detail, of experience, not poverty or war or sex or greed or race hatred, but the solipsistic condition of the human mind, which he regarded not as a pathology restricted to certain social classes, but as a universal human failing.

Crane's legacy to American letters, therefore, is one of style more than theme. This influence can be recognized, for example, in these sentences from Hemingway's *The Sun Also Rises* (1926):

> In the square a man, bent over, was playing on a reed-pipe, and a crowd of children were following him shouting, and pulling at his clothes. . . . We saw his blank pockmarked face as he went by, piping, the children close behind him shouting and pulling at him.
>
> "He must be the village idiot," Bill said.

Here, thirty years earlier, is Crane in "The Monster," describing a group of children gawking at the mutilated black man who has saved one of them from fire at cost to himself of his human features. He has become (in a story admired by Ralph Ellison) literally a creature without a face:

> Little Jimmie and many companions came around the corner of the stable. They were all in what was popularly known as the baby class, and consequently escaped from school a half-hour before the other children. They halted abruptly at sight of the figure on the box. Jimmie waved his hand with the air of a proprietor.
>
> "There he is," he said.

Crane's descriptive austerity in such passages was a form of resistance to what he deemed to be the human predilection for turning phenomena into symbols. If there is a Christian action anywhere in Crane's work, it is this black man's effort to save a child. Yet his scars are read not as stigmata but as marks of Cain. There was, finally, a difference between William James's account of mind and Crane's. For James, the capacity of the mind to formulate new truths under the pressure of new experience (for example, to discover that black men can be heroic) was the measure of man's freedom and his improvisatory genius. For Crane, by contrast, the productions of the mind are generally bad jokes at the expense of the observer and the observed: "The dead man and the living man exchanged a long look," he writes early in *The Red Badge of Courage*, bringing characteristically into focus what might be termed the junction between visual experience and the will to believe. There is, of course, no exchange here at all. It is language that makes the relation between living and dead seem reciprocal, and it is such fanciful language that becomes, for Crane, not the guarantor of truth, but its enemy.

This sort of enmity, as Edmund Wilson pointed out, had already taken hold in the American literary imagination well before the turn of the century, in the clean-swept prose of John W. De Forest, Ambrose Bierce, and many others (including Ulysses S. Grant, in his memoirs). Though Crane had no idea about war before he wrote *The Red Badge of Courage*, he touched many readers who had endured the real thing. His writing was so persuasive that one veteran, when the question arose of whether the author had served in the army at all, insisted that "I was with Crane at Antietam." The battle as narrated in the novel does conform in some respects to the events at Chancellorsville in 1863,

but the real secret of Crane's verisimilitude was his banishment
of abstractions. He gave a sense of war as a rush of smoke, din,
pus, flesh turned to pulp, as an experience entirely devoid of politics or purpose.

If the sound and sight of the flapping flag are sometimes huge
in Henry Fleming's consciousness, the socially inscribed meaning
of the flag is quite outside his understanding. It is merely a stick
from which a bit of cloth is suspended—sometimes one runs with
it, sometimes toward it, sometimes away from it, depending on
the direction in which instinct surges. The enemy is not a seces-
sionist, or a slavemaster, or an ideologue of any kind; he is merely
a faceless "brown swarm" from which death comes. Crane had
absolutely "no interest in the causes, meaning, or outcome of the
war," as John Berryman once put it. Yet the power of his novel
derived precisely from its refusal to traffic in the traditional vocabulary with which the Civil War had been represented. For
Crane, the war was not an "irrepressible conflict" (William Seward's phrase) or an event under the direction of "superintending
providence" (James Buchanan's). It is because Crane's readers
had been so saturated with such high-flown piety, I suspect, that
they took eagerly to his astringent version of events.

Crane's contempt for the platitudes of his culture gave him
what critical edge he had. He once stood up publicly, at risk to
his reputation, for a chorus girl who had been unjustly arrested
for streetwalking. He also wrote a story that elicited from the New
York City police commissioner at the time, Theodore Roosevelt,
the avuncular comment that "someday I want you to write another
story of the frontiersman and the Mexican Greaser in which the
frontiersman shall come out on top; it is more normal that way!"
Yet Crane was no reformer. His interest in prostitutes and gun-

slingers was hardly the Progressive's concern for the maladjusted. It was, instead, an attraction to those who cut through the palaver of bourgeois hypocrisy and got right to the point.

Crane's letters shed some light on this aspect of his mentality— in his epistolary courtship of Nellie Crouse, for example, which begins in the chivalric mode but dries up into matter-of-fact propositions, and eventually gives way before the greater appeal of Cora Stewart, proprietress of the Hotel de Dream, who knew something about love as a business. But the letters give surprisingly little help on some more vexing questions about Crane's career—on the problem, for instance, of which version of *The Red Badge of Courage* should be called authentic.

Along with Melville's *Typee* and Dreiser's *Sister Carrie, The Red Badge of Courage* has now become an American classic whose variant texts are significantly at odds with one another. There is some reason to believe that the famous last sentence of the novel ("Over the river a golden ray of sun came through the hosts of leaden rain clouds") may have been coaxed out of him by his publisher and was one of many such surrenders to propriety and phony emotion. Since the publication in 1982 of a text fully based on the manuscript, however, we have two *Red Badges*: one that was never published in Crane's lifetime and some scholars claim was the book he meant to write, another that is replete with such embellishments as the final sunburst (the book we have known since Appleton published it in 1895). Unfortunately, the letters tell us little that helps decide between the two, a situation that is, perhaps, in accord with Crane's likely attitude toward such questions: one sees what one prefers.

The real poignancy of Crane's work and life is the wistfulness beneath the iconoclasm. His ferocity against the pieties of his culture, which is most evident in his gnomic poems, conceals a reluctance to give them up. He was like a child protesting boredom on the sidelines of a babyish game—belief—that he wants to play but is afraid, for fear of embarrassment, to join. When Crane died, he was at work on an unpromising novel about an Irishman in England. Henry James wrote to his widow, "I think of him with such a sense of possibilities and powers!" But Crane, unlike James himself, distrusted the imagination, which is why James was off the mark—or gallantly consolatory—with his implicit prediction that there would have been much more.

7

Was Kate Chopin a Feminist?

It seems a long time ago that teachers could distribute without embarrassment *The Lifetime Reading Plan* or some such guide to literacy and expect students to measure their progress toward adulthood by the number of checks beside the titles read. There is a certain comfort in the authority of lists. But since we may never again have such lists, the idea of the classic—if it is to be preserved at all—needs to be saved from the idea of the absolute. In a charming rescue operation conducted some years ago, Frank Kermode gave this modest definition of what a classic is: "A classic . . . is a book that is read a long time after it was written."

It is now nearly a century since *The Awakening* was written—a once obscure, now famous, novel of adultery and suicide by Kate Chopin. Born into a well-to-do St. Louis family in 1851, Kate O'Flaherty married at the age of nineteen a prosperous New Orleans merchant named Oscar Chopin, who died twelve years later, leaving her a widow in her early thirties. It was under these conditions that she began to write stories.

The reputation of the one novel Kate Chopin published, *The*

Awakening, has fluctuated from scandal when it first appeared in 1899 and was angrily received as an American *Madame Bovary* to near-oblivion during the first half of the twentieth century until Cyrille Arnavon translated it into French and Robert Cantwell and Edmund Wilson began to reclaim it for our own literature. According to my last count, it was in print in sixteen editions competing for the college and high school market.

During its long dormancy, *The Awakening* did manage to survive in scholarly histories as an example of regionalism or "local color." To be designated a work of "regionalism" was, not too long ago, to be dismissed as provincial, but one reason *The Awakening* is now a classroom staple is that "local" has become an honorific term. If it once implied limits and smallness, the word "local" now suggests integrity, purity, and resistance to a malevolent power often referred to in academic circles as the "center." I want briefly to consider this strange new geography of value before turning to the novel itself.

One representative critic, Marjorie Pryse, puts the matter clearly:

> The belief in universals has [too long] held its own in the face of attacks by what we might collectively term regional interests: black studies and the civil rights movement, women's studies and the resurgence of feminism, American studies and a return to grassroots politics, as well as movements for gay rights, Native American heritage, and so on. Therefore, a reevaluation of regional concepts must begin by accounting for the pervasive undermining of "local" concerns and texts by the conviction the majority of citizens in the culture share that there do indeed exist "universals."

Reclaiming the regional tradition amounts, in this view, to an act of solidarity with the excluded, the oppressed, the "marginalized."

It may, however, be worth enlarging the question of why regionalism has lately enjoyed academic revival by looking beyond the sphere of literary study. As recently as thirty years ago in the United States, "the revision of accepted standards of cultural value" (Pryse's phrase) chiefly meant revision of such "universals" as these: race hatred, indifference toward the poor, and tolerance of prevailing conditions in the industrial workplace. Moreover, the revision of these accepted standards was carried out not regionally but from Washington, the nation's center of political power.

In what is surely a conspicuous irony, the language of antagonism toward the "center" has become, in the last twenty years or so, the shared property of the political right and the academic left. One remembers, for instance, that Richard Nixon often invoked the formula that it was "time for power to stop flowing from the people to the capital, and to start flowing from the capital to the people," a kind of talk that became more common in the 1980s and 1990s (even as I write, the responsibility for millions of needy children is being redistributed, through the process of welfare "reform," to "local" authorities) and is the leading language of cultural criticism as well. The leftish academy celebrates regionalism as an assault on what it decries as the pernicious "norms" of American ideology (patriarchy, laissez-faire capitalism, imperial expansion), while the political right invokes the idea of regional autonomy as a way to restore those very norms under new names: "family values," entrepreneurship, national defense. If regionalism is in good odor among both professors and politicians, perhaps we ought to wonder if the gap between the academic left and the political right is as wide as both sides like to claim.

*   *   *

With this question in mind, what does one make of *The Awak-ening*, whose transformation from a work of local interest into a prestigious novel has been rivaled only by Zora Neale Hurston's *Their Eyes Were Watching God*? This book does not fit within any of the customary ideological categories. Anyone who has dis-cussed it in the classroom knows that it can be read with assent by readers of quite opposite convictions on issues of sexual poli-tics. This story of a frantically unhappy woman sets itself off from the usual regional evocation of the sexually awakened country girl—as Hamlin Garland described her, for example, in his col-lection of sketches about life in the Midwest, *Main-Travelled Roads* (1891):

> "Girls in love ain't no use in the whole blessed week," she
> said. "Sundays they're a-lookin' down the road, expectin' he'll
> *come*. Sunday afternoons they can't think o' nothin' else,
> 'cause he's *here*. Monday mornin's they're sleepy and kind
> dreamy and slimpsy, and good f'r nothin' on Tuesday and
> Wednesday. Thursday they git absent-minded, an' begin to
> look off toward Sunday agin, an' mope aroun' and let the
> dishwater git cold, right under their noses. Friday they break
> dishes, and go off in the best room an' snivel, an' look out o'
> the winder. Saturdays, they have queer spurts o' working' like
> all p'sessed, an' spurts o' frizzin' their hair. An' Sunday they
> begin it all over agin."

This Midwestern Penelope is not yet grown into an adult capable of stratagem, but she is on her way to becoming the eternally untarnished wife, a human exemplar of the fertile land in which she makes her life, or, more accurately, in which she performs her service. She is what Carrie Meeber would have been if she had stayed in rural Wisconsin and never boarded the train for Chicago.

The tormented wife and mother of *The Awakening*, Edna Pontellier, is entirely different. The daughter of a Kentucky Presbyterian who "atone[s] for his weekday sins with his Sunday devotions," Edna marries into the dying French Catholic culture of New Orleans, where, even at the end of the nineteenth century, women were still living virtually without rights under a version of the Napoleonic legal code. In this static world she becomes a sort of captive ambassador from the frontier country in which she had been born—and an object of flirtatious interest among the quasi-Frenchmen of New Orleans.

These men are of a recognizable sort in turn-of-the-century American fiction. One may think not only of Henry James's ineffectual males ("Young men are very different from what I was," says the elder Mr. Touchett in *The Portrait of a Lady* [1881], "when I cared for a girl—when I was young—I wanted to do more than look at her") but of Dreiser's Hurstwood in *Sister Carrie* descending through shabbiness into despair, or of Stephen Crane's boy-soldier in *The Red Badge of Courage* trying to prove himself on the battlefield, or, a little later, of this complaint from Mrs. Bart in Edith Wharton's *The House of Mirth* (1905): "It had been among that lady's grievances that her husband [whose bankruptcy and death have left the family groping for position] in the early days, before he was too tired, had wasted his evenings in what she vaguely described as 'reading poetry.'" If the literary record can be trusted, America at the turn of the century seems to have been populated by men who could not cope.

Kate Chopin agreed. She witnessed in New Orleans what Wharton saw in New York and what another "regionalist," the New England writer Sarah Orne Jewett, saw in coastal Maine: a once haughty privileged class on the edge of extinction, nominally led by men too shriveled to lead. Edna's first infatuation, Robert Lebrun, brings his "high voice" and "serio-comic" charm each summer to the tony resort at Grand Isle, where he constitutes "himself the devoted attendant of some fair dame or damsel . . . sometimes a young girl, [or] a widow . . . [or] some interesting married woman." He seems best pleased as a kind of humored troubadour sitting at the feet of an unavailable lady. From this posture he recites titillating accounts of his amorous adventures, and is excited in turn by "the lady at the needle [who] kept up a little running, contemptuous comment: *"Blagueur—farceur— gros bête, va!'* " There is a hint of sexual self-abasement here, but in the end such entertainments on even the hottest Louisiana nights feel more filial than carnal. This man has fallen out of the active world. He has become something between a jester and a gigolo.

So male attenuation is one theme Chopin shared with other regional writers of her time. Jewett populated her *Country of the Pointed Firs* (1896) with men who are either drifting into senility or frozen in boyhood, keeping about them "a remote and juvenile sort of silence." But whereas Jewett gives us a settled psychic condition as a consequence of New England's economic decline (her men languish in a kind of melancholy reverie about the past), Chopin shows us a Southern version of the same problem as social *process*—a process she makes visible by giving us glimpses of Creole men who are mainly devoted to dissipation. Robert, whose voice Edna finds so "musical and true," leaves suddenly for Mexico with no evident itinerary. Alcée Arobin, whose "good figure [and] pleasing face" console her after Robert's departure by "appealing to the animalism that stirred impatiently within her," has no evident vocation—except to be her second conquest.

As Edna ventures further from her husband, she finds herself, sometimes literally, on a border between old and new. "I saw her," reports Dr. Mandelet, ". . . walking along Canal Street"— the dividing line between the French Quarter and the modern city that was outgrowing the historic New Orleans boundaries. Her house, dressed and painted "a dazzling white" to please the scanning eye, is an expression of the old Creole femininity as a self-advertising bauble. Graceful, glad to be owned, its "round, fluted columns support the sloping roof." But it is also Edna's prison. Chopin conveys the sense of confinement from the first sentence of the novel, which presents "a green and yellow parrot . . . hung in a cage," making imitative sounds to the amusement of visitors.

When she gets an occasional furlough, the place where Edna most likes to spend her free moments is the home of Mademoiselle Reisz, whose "apartments up under the roof" are high above the world of noise and barter. "There were plenty of windows in [Mademoiselle Reisz's] little front room. They were for the most part dingy, but as they were nearly always open it did not make so much difference . . . From her windows could be seen the crescent of the river, the masts of ships and the big chimneys of the Mississippi steamers." If Edna's house is all surfaces, the home of Mademoiselle Reisz has an interior genuinely expressive of its owner, but also bravely open to the world.

Much of the novel is concerned with Edna's attempt to learn something from this example. She struggles to open her mind to the meaning of the appurtenances—some chosen, some not—

among which she must live out her life. To put it another way, she begins to understand that she can at least modify the scenes of her existence. Rooms, views, streets, furnishings—in the full sense of the word, "decor"—are a realm of experience whose significance had once been lost on her. Now that she begins to distinguish between the life assigned to her and the possibility of fashioning herself anew, she makes her boldest (and most often quoted) declaration: "I would give up the unessential; I would give away my money, I would give my life for my children; but I wouldn't give myself." With this series of renunciations, she has come to sense the existence of a free and irreducible self.

But what constitutes this self? What can be discarded as "unessential"? Edna's first hint of an answer, as she rises out of her appointed role as imported wife, is her discovery that self-awareness begins with the sense of touch:

Edna, left alone in the little side room, loosened her clothes, removing the greater part of them. She bathed her face, her neck and arms in the basin that stood between the windows. She took off her shoes and stockings and stretched herself in the very center of the high, white bed. How luxurious it felt to rest thus in a strange, quaint bed, with its sweet country odor of laurel lingering about the sheets and mattress! She stretched her strong limbs that ached a little. She ran her fingers through her loosened hair for a while. She looked at her round arms, as she held them straight up and rubbed them one after the other, observing closely, as if it were something she saw for the first time, the fine, firm quality and texture of her flesh. She clasped her hands easily above her head, and it was thus she fell asleep.

Complaining that he meets his wife now only "at breakfast," Mr. Pontellier has no role in his wife's sexual awakening, but neither exactly does the flirtatious Robert, who seems poised to supplant him as her partner: Robert's "face [grows] a little white" when she gives him a glimpse of her aroused sexuality. Even Arobin, though less hesitant to test his capacity to slake her desire, is more voyeur than lover. In thwarted pursuit of partnership, Edna grows more and more lonely. Whenever she hears her friend Mademoiselle Reisz play a certain plaintive piano melody (though she knows that "the name of the piece was something else") she calls it "Solitude," and imagines "the figure of a man standing [naked] beside a desolate rock on the seashore." She is haunted by this image of a single figure interrupting an unpeopled vista. Her situation calls to mind that wicked rejoinder spoken by Marilyn Monroe at the opening of Arthur Miller's screenplay for *The Misfits*: The devastated young husband, just discarded on the courthouse steps after signing the divorce papers, begs her to say why she wants to leave him. "If I have to be alone," she replies, "I'd rather be by myself."

Edna, too, refuses to be part of her husband's bric-a-brac and begins to create an environment of her own invention—a process that begins in earnest with her husband's departure for New York on business. As the day for his leaving draws near, she scurries about the house in a new kind of agitation—guilty, we suspect, not so much over remaining without him as over her premonition of the temptations of independence. "She was solicitous about his health and his welfare. She bustled around, looking after his clothing, thinking about heavy underwear . . ." Nearly twenty-nine, she behaves like a child of sixteen whose conscience acts up in anticipation of a weekend without supervision. But when she is at last left alone, relief conquers guilt, and she tours "her" house with a combination of proprietorship and sensory excitement:

> A feeling that was unfamiliar but very delicious came over her. She walked all through the house, from one room to another, as if inspecting it for the first time. She tried the various chairs and lounges, as if she had never sat and reclined upon them before. And she perambulated around the outside of the house, investigating, looking to see if windows and shutters were secure and in order. The flowers were like new acquaintances; she approached them in a familiar spirit, and made herself at home among them. The garden walks were damp, and Edna called to the maid to bring out her rubber sandals. And there she stayed, and stooped, digging around the plants, trimming, picking dead, dry leaves. The children's little dog came out, interfering, getting in her way. She scolded him, laughing at him, played with him. The garden smelled so good and looked so pretty in the afternoon sunlight. Edna plucked all the bright flowers she could find, and went into the house with them, she and the little dog.

This is a passage into discovery but not, I suspect, an introduction to self-knowledge. Edna's mood of release at her husband's departure, which begins as involuntary exultation, quickly becomes conscious and strategic, until she takes the first step toward remaking her life. She will, she decides, move out of the big house into a cottage around the block. "Just two steps away," she tells Mademoiselle Reisz, who has challenged her for an explanation. "I'm tired of looking after that big house. It never seemed like mine, anyway—like home." As Mademoiselle Reisz senses, the key word is "mine"; Edna is developing a taste for ownership. She falls into pecuniary explanations:

> Oh! I see there is no deceiving you. Then let me tell you: It is a caprice. I have a little money of my own from my mother's estate, which my father sends to me by driblets. I won a large sum this winter on the races, and I am beginning to sell my sketches.

It is now possible to see why Chopin has used a teasing, ironic sentence to mark the moment when the novel shifts from the open spaces of Grand Isle to the interiors of New Orleans: "The Pontelliers possessed a charming home on Esplanade Street." Strictly speaking, Edna—as distinct from her husband—possesses nothing. As Margaret Culley, one of the modern editors of *The Awakening*, has pointed out about the Louisiana legal code, "all of a wife's 'accumulations' after marriage were the property of her husband, including money she might earn and the clothes she wore." Yet Chopin implies that in a larger sense Edna is becoming an equal partner in the plural subject ("the Pontelliers") of her sentence. She is becoming a possessor. She has begun to escape the condition of being (or at least learning to be) a proper Creole lady. But it is not sufficient to speak of what she is leaving behind. To come fully to terms with this novel, we must follow Edna into the terrible limbo into which she now falls. By the time of her husband's departure, *The Awakening* has become a book about her suspension not merely between Kentucky Presbyterianism and Creole Catholicism, or between halves of the city divided by Canal Street, but between the genders themselves.

This transformation has been hinted from the start. "She was rather handsome than beautiful," we are told early, and before long she learns to drink "liquor from the glass as a man would have done." This most basic of the novel's suspensions—between femininity and masculinity as forms of social being—takes a predictably large psychic toll. Edna's statement that "I am beginning to sell my sketches," for instance, is a check on her emerging artistic commitment, which is explicitly associated with female dissent from the male world of commodity display and exchange. Surely her moment of highest self-realization comes when she is able—like her friends Madame Ratignolle (with her children) and Mademoiselle Reisz (with her music)—to take pleasure in the intrinsic value of something she has produced. Edna "had reached a stage [with her painting] where she seemed to be no longer feeling her way, working, when in the humor, with sureness and ease. And being devoid of ambition, and striving not toward accomplishment, she drew satisfaction from the work in itself."

In Chopin's world, this experience is unavailable or, more accurately, unaffordable for men. Edna's brush with it is one of those moments when it is useful to think of *The Awakening* in roughly Marxian terms: she has escaped, at least momentarily, from alienation. Even if it is only a fleeting freedom, she conceives, for a moment, of neither her work nor herself as a commodity—which is why "I am beginning to sell my sketches" is double-edged. What in one sense is the beginning of independent professionalism—a feminist victory—is also a lapse into equating the expression of self with marketable goods and services. Edna, who has been bought and sold, is entering the marketplace as a vendor.

Both aspects of this awakening—liberation and constriction— are adumbrated in the brilliant account of her father's visit. Once a proud colonel in the Confederate Army, he sits "before her pencil . . . rigid and unflinching, as he had faced the cannon's mouth in days gone by." This is, if ever there was one, a phallic pencil: an emblem of daughterly usurpation. "Her lack of filial kindness and respect" is not excused by the scrutiny to which she subjects him while making his portrait. When she refuses to attend her sister's wedding, he accuses her of further deficiencies: a "want of sisterly and womanly consideration." As both Mademoiselle Reisz and Madame Ratignolle realize, Edna is replacing her thralldom to men in general and to particular men—father, husband, imagined lovers—with the thrill of partaking in exactly the experience that they had once monopolized: the experience of power.

This exchange of roles creates the conditions for her self-destruction:

"Take the fan," said Edna, offering it to [Robert].
"Oh, no! Thank you. It does no good; you have to stop fanning some time, and feel all the more uncomfortable afterward."
"That is one of the ridiculous things which men always say. I have never known one to speak otherwise of fanning."

Mocking Robert for the calculus of pain and pleasure that he applies to the most trivial choices, Edna has had enough of computation; enough, when she wants to linger outside in the night, of her husband's "you will take cold out there." To fan or not to fan, she suggests, is a pathetic question. Edna is learning a new language of impulse that is explicitly identified as female, at least within the universe of the novel, and this is precisely why it is so ominous when she falls back, like the caged parrot, into mimicry: "I hardly think we need new fixtures, Léonce," she says to her husband. "Don't let us get anything new: you are too extravagant. I don't believe you ever think of saving or putting by." Such spousal scolding is a fair imitation of her husband's nagging.

Edna's "awakening" never wholly renovates her consciousness. She "never awakens," as Elaine Showalter has pointed out, "to the dimensions of her social world . . . never sees how the labor of the mulatto and black women around her makes her narcissistic existence possible." Because of the servants, she is able to keep the world of her children at a muted distance: "The boys were being put to bed; the patter of their bare, escaping feet could be heard occasionally, as well as the pursuing voice of the quadroon." The children's life upstairs is a bit of background noise. Edna exists in a relation to governess and children not very different from her husband's relation to her, as a remote employer. "If one of the little Pontellier boys took a tumble whilst at play, he was not apt to rush crying to his mother's arms for comfort; he would more likely pick himself up, wipe the water out of his eyes and the sand out of his mouth, and go on playing." Childbirth itself is something she had once barely apprehended through an anesthetic haze. And the numbness lingers not only in memory but as a "stupor which had deadened sensation," and which, despite the novel's title (chosen, we should recall, by the publisher, not the author), closes tighter and tighter around her as her "awakening" proceeds: "She felt no interest in anything about her. The street, the children, the fruit vender, the flowers growing there under her eyes, were all part and parcel of an alien world." Sensory deprivation is another point toward which she converges in company with the men around her. Léonce sits at their dining table pouring "pepper, salt, vinegar, mustard—everything within reach" into his soup, in the hope of giving it some bite. He and Edna are not so much an opposition as a matched pair.

But if Edna and her husband descend together into dull discontent, they differ in how they cope with the death-in-life they share. For him the only release is to carry on his business, to make the pretense that nothing is off-center in his life. For Edna, the resort is to sex:

> She leaned over and kissed [Robert]—a soft, cool, delicate kiss, whose voluptuous sting penetrated his whole being— then she moved away from him. . . . She took his face between her hands and looked into it as if she would never withdraw her eyes more.

Granting to Edna this control over the rhythm of penetration and withdrawal, Chopin takes her still further away from "femininity." Squeamish Robert is appalled. "Foolish boy," Edna calls him, and declares herself "no longer one of Mr. Pontellier's possessions. . . . I give myself where I choose." As Robert declines to receive this gift, *The Awakening* becomes one of those books devoted to exposing the male fear of female sexuality, a fear that runs deep through American culture, from drawing-room magazines such as *Godey's Lady's Book* to the *Playboy* airbrush. Robert cannot abide what F. Scott Fitzgerald was later to call the "ghastly reiterated female sound" of a woman's orgasm.

Arobin is more willing to parry Edna's thrusts. Yet there is no fulfillment in her intimacy with him. Using the language of pa-

thology, Chopin remarks that "the excitement [of Arobin's pres-
ence] came back upon her like a remittent fever." She acquaints
Edna with desire not only for men but for drink, for gambling,
for anything that will heat her blood. It is an appetite of which
Edna is aware to the point of fear:

> "Will you go to the races again?" he asked.
>
> "No," she said. "I've had enough of the races. I don't want
> to lose all the money I've won, and I've got to work when
> the weather is bright, instead of—"
>
> "Yes; work; to be sure. You promise to show me your work.
> What morning may I come up to your atelier? To-morrow?"
>
> "No!"
>
> "Day after?"
>
> "No, no."
>
> "Oh, please don't refuse me! I know nothing of such
> things. I might help you with a stray suggestion or two."
>
> "No. Good night. Why don't you go after you have said good
> night?" I don't like you," she went on in a high, excited pitch,
> attempting to draw away her hand. She felt that her words
> lacked dignity and sincerity, and she knew that he felt it.

Arobin has attached himself to her not with anything resembling
love, but with an anthropological interest in a woman who has
put away her husband, who paints, and who plays the horses like
a man. She knows that his patronizing visit to her studio would
contaminate her. She does not want to paint for the likes of him,
to be beholden to him; and as their confrontation comes to its
manifold climax, she pays a high price for her excitement:

". . . I can tell what manner of woman you are." His fingers strayed occasionally down to her warm, smooth cheeks and firm chin, which was growing a little full and double.

"Oh, yes! You will tell me that I am adorable; everything that is captivating. Spare yourself the effort."

"No; I shan't tell you anything of the sort, though I shouldn't be lying if I did."

"Do you know Mademoiselle Reisz?" she asked irrelevantly . . .

"I'm told she's extremely disagreeable and unpleasant. Why have you introduced her at a moment when I desired to talk of you?"

Edna has, of course, introduced Mademoiselle Reisz not "irrelevantly" at all, but as a last shield against him. Work and sex are explicitly countervailed at this critical moment—just as they are in a number of Chopin's best stories ("Wiser Than a God" [1889], "Aunt Lympy's Interference" [1897]) that document a woman's refusal to give up her vocation for a sexual attachment. Arobin, Edna knows, is nothing more than a measure of her desperation to find an antidote to numbness.

He is, however, no fool. He chides her with wicked aptness about her plan to hold a *fête* in honor of her leaving the old house: "What about the dinner," he asked, "the grand event, the *coup d'état*?" His phrasing cannot be improved upon, for it drives home the point that Edna's is to be a revolution in incidentals only. Nothing, Arobin implies, will change except the identity of the ruler, a proposition with which Chopin appears to agree: "There was something in her attitude, in her whole appearance when she leaned her head against the high-backed chair and spread her arms, which suggested the regal woman, the one who rules, who looks on, who stands alone." With Mademoiselle Reisz propped on a cushioned chair as if in proxy for Edna's absent children, the whole affair has an air of unintentional self-mockery. Edna sits alone, presiding at a childless table while her lover undergoes interrogation by the one man present who speaks for the *ancien régime*—Monsieur Ratignolle. This is one of the great sad parties in American literature. It ranks with the Touchetts' tea at Gardencourt (in *The Portrait of a Lady*) and the revels on Gatsby's lawn. After this *coup d'état* (Edna takes possession of her "pigeon house" upon her thirtieth birthday), the rest of the novel is a long coda.

What makes the final pages of *The Awakening* so painful is their accumulating sense that Edna is living with foreknowledge of her doom. She sputters in sentences that start and stall and start again. She tells Dr. Mandelet:

> There are periods of despondency and suffering which take possession of me. But I don't want anything but my own way. That is wanting a good deal, of course, when you have to trample upon the lives, the prejudices of others—but no matter—still, I shouldn't want to trample upon the little lives. Oh! I don't know what I'm saying, Doctor. Good night. Don't blame me for anything.

It was this kind of self-exoneration that offended Chopin's first readers. Edna has lost a battle that, according to the respectable opinion of her time, she should never have begun. She has lost her fight against ennui and, what is worse, she knows it: "There was no one thing in the world that she desired. There was no human being whom she wanted near her except Robert; and she even realized that the day would come when he, too, and the thought of him would melt out of her existence, leaving her alone." Her walk into the sea delivers her from a limbo that Chopin is at pains to liken to that of the mulatto woman in whose home Edna takes refuge: " 'Do you come here often?' Robert asked, in the woman's garden. 'I almost live here,' Edna answered."

This bitter remark tells what sort of book *The Awakening* finally becomes. Edna's flight from her condition as her husband's possession is strikingly akin to what one encounters in many turn-of-the-century novels that take the predicament of the mulatto as their main theme. These books are built on a tragic paradox: that the only hope for the fugitive is to become indistinguishable from those from whom she is in flight.

One well-known example of such a novel is Charles Chesnutt's *The House Behind the Cedars* (1900), a book that attacks the premises of racism (as *The Awakening* does the idea of woman's "proper place") by demonstrating the danger of revealed genealogy. Like *The Awakening*, it is a meditation on how the sex or color of the body with which one is born becomes an ineffaceable sign of one's obligation and worth. "One drop of black blood makes the whole man black," says one of the many bigots in Chesnutt's novel, and we cringe, much as we do when Mr. Pontellier rattles off the time-honored proscriptions that Edna is beginning to defy. Yet the suspense of Chesnutt's novel builds as the white lover stumbles close to the discovery that there is "black blood" in the veins of his beloved. Holding our breath as we follow her efforts to conceal this fact from him, we become complicit in a strategy that amounts to a repudiation of her past. The naming of blackness in such a book becomes a drifting illusion: a woman is black only if someone knows it, only if (in the phrase of an earlier novelist, William Wells Brown) "the melting mezzotinto" in the iris of her eye is noticed. I suspect that this reduction of black identity to an epistemological riddle goes some distance toward explaining why Chesnutt spent the last thirty years of his life in literary silence.

Except for a few stories and reviews, Chopin, too, fell silent before her writing life seemed ready to end. She died in 1904 without producing or even embarking on a work comparable in ambition to *The Awakening*. In her earlier work she had been explicitly concerned with the mulatto theme only rarely, notably in her well-known story "Désirée's Baby." Yet surely it is no accident that Edna seeks refuge in a mulatto woman's home. We wish Edna free. We shudder at her confinement and thrill to her release. But her "awakening" leaves her mimicking the social instincts of those who have suppressed her in the first place. Just as the "ex-colored" awaken one day to find themselves irredeemably white, she becomes what she once fled.

In other words, Edna recognizes in her "awakening" a new form of degradation. She swims to her death not, as some readers would like to imagine, in a kind of ecstatic suicide amid the warm Gulf waves, but in despair at not having found a third way between the alternatives of submission and emulation when faced by those who regard power as the ground of all human relations.

8

Lyrical Dreiser

"In this republican country, amid the fluctuating waves of our social life," Nathaniel Hawthorne wrote in *The House of the Seven Gables* (1851), "somebody is always at the drowning-point." It was not the deprivation of the poor that interested Hawthorne, but rather the fall of those born high—the experience of failure. Like most of his contemporaries, Hawthorne did not look closely at the conspicuous castaways of antebellum America. Even to Melville, the face of social misery tended to be a foreign one. When he wrote in *Redburn* of his back-alley encounter with "the figure of what had been a woman . . . [in whose] blue arms [were] folded to her livid bosom two shrunken things like children," he was writing about the desperate poor of Liverpool, not New York.

Among post–Civil War writers, Theodore Dreiser was the first to write powerfully about the experience rather than the spectacle of poverty. He did not have to acquaint himself with the subject. Born in Terre Haute in 1871 to a pious Catholic millworker who had fled the Prussian draft and an American-born mother of Moravian descent, he was, F. O. Matthiessen has remarked, "the first

major American writer whose family name was not English or
Scotch Irish." Dreiser grew up in a crowded household; there
were five boys and five girls born over a period of fifteen years,
of whom Theodore was the second youngest. The children's ventures outside the family tested the tolerance of their father, whom
Dreiser remembered in his memoir, *Dawn* (1931), "as a kind of
pleading watchdog of the treasury, weeping in his beard and
moaning over the general recklessness of our lives."

There was reason for the elder Dreiser's worry. His first son,
Paul, was arrested in his teens for robbing a saloon; another,
Rome, became known about town as a bouncer and a thug.
Among the girls, Mame began to collect from prominent male
citizens presents that ranged from trinkets to cash, while Emma
and the darkly beautiful Sylvia, as Dreiser's biographer Richard
Lingeman puts it, "bartered their youth to rich older men in return for the trappings of luxury without the legitimization of marriage."

Theodore's sisters called him "big-eared" owing to both his un-
gainliness and his attentiveness to their affairs. For Theodore,
these sisters—especially Emma and Sylvia, whom "for reasons of
temperament I class together"—were the first to hint at the
"stinging richness" of adult life. They were, he wrote, "a pair of
idlewilds, driven helplessly and persistently by their own internal
fires." He remembered Sylvia especially "as nearly always before
her mirror, rouging her cheeks and lips, darkening her eyebrows
and lashes . . . feeling her waist and hips to see if they were trim
enough." Adornments were unnecessary, since men flocked to her
whether she made herself up or not: a sweet-talking shoe sales-
man nearly coaxed her onto the next train; a tightrope walker in
town for a carnival dazzled her in his "varicolored fleshings and

gorgeous velvet loin cloths"; even "a certain Professor Solax"—
one of those traveling quacks of the period that L. Frank Baum
had in mind for the Wizard of Oz—"a small, trim, dandified man,
in a cutaway coat and high silk hat, with shoebrush whiskers and
Jovian curls," begged her to run away with him. "And while his
curly hair and amazing whiskers were entrancing enough, she
feared that he had a wife somewhere (by this time this had come
to mean an obstacle to her) and she did not go."

When in his twenties Dreiser, after his apprenticeship as a journalist, undertook to become a novelist, it was out of such scraps
of his sisters' lives that he fashioned his two first novels, *Sister
Carrie* (1900) and *Jennie Gerhardt* (1911). Dreiser continued to
write fiction for another thirty years, producing a remarkable tril-
ogy—the Cowperwood novels (1912–47)—about a tycoon who
combines ruthlessness with grandeur, like the cities he conquers
(first Philadelphia, then Chicago). *An American Tragedy* (1925),
in its sheer narrative drive, is perhaps Dreiser's best book. But
Sister Carrie and *Jennie Gerhardt*, in their emotional intensity,
are the most intimate and lyrical.

These books are in large part imaginative revisions of his sisters'
lives with many of the facts intact: the old immigrant Gerhardt
rails at Jennie for what he considers her loose morals, as Dreiser's
father had done at his wayward daughters; around the most scandalous episode of Emma's life—her flight to Canada with a married lover who had embezzled money from his employers—
Dreiser built the plot of *Sister Carrie*.

Theodore himself had brushes with trouble, but he learned how
to evade the trainmen and the police while scrambling for coal as
a boy in the railroad yards of Terre Haute. His was, in many
respects, the classic late-nineteenth-century childhood of the poor

immigrant's son—the restless New World boy struggling against the restrictions of an Old World father. John Paul Dreiser had been a master weaver in Germany, but in the United States he could never turn his tradesman's skill into a business success. He made bad investments, and grew too timid to try again; he was battered by the volatility of the American markets and was hurt by his loyalty, and caution, and pride.

The family spoke German at home, and at his father's insistence, Theodore was sent to a German-speaking parochial school—one reason why his sentences often reflect some discomfort with customary English word order. Dreiser also grew up Catholic in a Protestant country, "drilled in the wornout folderol of the Holy Roman Catholic Church," and subject to his father's rantings: "No Bible [in these American schools]; or if there is one, a Protestant Bible . . . full of lies! No separation of boys and girls as there should be in any well regulated state of society!" Lingeman is right to speak of "the oppressive fears" that Dreiser associated with Catholicism:

> At the elevation of the Host, so cowed was I by dogma that
> I invariably knelt, even behind the organ, not because I felt
> it to be so sacred or spiritual a moment but because of the
> fear that if I did not I might die in the act of committing a
> mortal sin and so be consigned to eternal fire.

Yet when Dreiser conceded that "much as I might dislike the routine of the Catholic Church, it was ever of interest to me as a spectacle," he may have been understating the hold it had over him.

Dreiser began to learn of the world through reading pulp magazines (*The Family Story Paper, The Fireside Companion*) and particularly through his brother Paul, who was embarking on a show-business career when Dreiser was growing up. Paul got his start in a Cincinnati minstrel show and eventually made his way East to become a Broadway songwriter and bon vivant—his most famous song was "On the Banks of the Wabash"—and, after long absences, he would come home on visits with perfumed women in high heels and with fabulous stories to tell. He changed his name to "Dresser" as "a concession to the American middle west . . . which thought little of all foreign names." During the early 1890s he lived for a while near the family in Evansville with the madam of a local brothel, an elegant woman whose "exotic taste for black" young Theodore explained to himself as a sign that she was in mourning.

Paul's charm and success compensated for his worldliness, even to his disapproving mother. Later in the decade, when Theodore first came to New York to try to become a writer, the two shared an apartment, in which Paul made a practice of parading up and down with a bath towel hung on his morning erection; Theodore remembered this as both a shock to his prudishness and an encouragement to his awakening sexuality. Paul became his younger brother's guide to the pleasures of New York, where he seemed "one of those great Falstaffian sorts who, for lack of a little iron or sodium or carbon dioxide in his chemical compost, was not able to bestride the world like a Colossus." A dashing figure (until he became hugely fat and ill from drinking), he introduced Theodore to exotic whorehouses and came indispensably to his aid when, in his early twenties, he fell into a serious mental depression.

After his brother's death, Dreiser reflected that he "belongs in a novel, which I shall never find the time to write." His vivid portrait in *Twelve Men*, written in 1909, shows Paul in all his "agile geniality" on drinking binges with cronies like the former Western con man Bat Masterson, the prizefighter James J. Corbett, and various luminaries of Tammany Hall. He describes Paul in New York hotels, entertaining crowds with his gift for mimicry—how he did the "old Irish washerwoman arguing; a stout, truculent German laying down the law; lean, gloomy, out-at-elbows actors of the Hamlet or classic school complaining of their fate; the stingy skinflint haggling over a dollar." But Paul is also a character in a Dreiser novel. Hurstwood in *Sister Carrie* has something of his charm and dandyism, and in the terrible symmetry of Paul's early success and abrupt decline and death (in 1906) Hurstwood's fall is strangely reenacted.

During Dreiser's childhood, the younger children moved frequently with their mother—to Evansville, Warsaw, Sullivan, to Chicago and back to Evansville—while their father stayed in Terre Haute and tried to earn a living. As Theodore entered what Lingeman calls "the glandular storms of adolescence," he drew away from the family and returned to Chicago, where, barely sixteen, he kept poverty at arm's length by working as a dishwasher, freight-car tracer, hardware stockpiler, real estate promoter, laundry-truck driver, bill collector—jobs, especially the last, that plunged him into the human chaos of the city. There his fantasies about willing women looking for young men to please were more than occasionally realized. "Plump wives drew me into risqué positions on sight." And there, too, began the lifelong struggle between his strong sexual urge and an almost equivalent sexual fear—fear of disease, of ineptness, of making a girl pregnant. "I have never known a man more interested in women from the sex point of view," he said of Paul, adding, "unless perchance it might be myself."

On his bill-collecting rounds he was stimulated imaginatively as well as physically. "Death-bereaved weepers mourned over their late lost in my presence—and postponed paying me." He was propositioned "by plump naked girls striding from bed to dresser to get a purse, [who] then offered certain favors for a dollar, or its equivalent—a credit on the contract slip." He began to think about writing it all down.

These adventures were interrupted when a former high school teacher from Warsaw, having noticed his gifts, talked him into entering Indiana University, at her expense. But Dreiser left Bloomington a year later, after his mother died, and went back to Chicago. There he began to knock on editors' doors looking for a job as a reporter, planting himself outside the newsroom, he later wrote in *Newspaper Days* (1922), like "a homeless cat hang[ing] about . . . meowing to be taken in." By sheer persistence and the luck of being around during the busy political season when papers needed stringers, he landed a paid-by-the-piece job at the Chicago *Daily Globe*. His first break came quickly, during the Democratic convention of 1892, when he gave his paper a scoop on the impending nomination of Grover Cleveland.

But the main story of Dreiser's early years as a reporter, first in Chicago, then in St. Louis and, briefly, in Pittsburgh, is his discovery that he was not a newsman but a writer. Dreiser's gift as a reporter was not for ferreting out tips and late-breaking stories but for gathering impressions. At the St. Louis *Globe-Democrat* he hit his stride with a column called "Heard in the Corridors," which mixed invention with interviews and barroom chatter, and turned them into vignettes. There are sketches of a restaurant that managed to fleece tourists without raising prices for its regular customers by slicing the tourists' steaks thinner; of a paralytic who had been buried alive; of a smoker who bled to death from a sore on his lip. He wrote Sunday-supplement features (about revival meetings, visits to the morgue, local fairs, baseball games). Dreiser was training his ear and eye for the salient detail—the regional lilt of a voice, the fashionable cut of a suit.

He became known, in the words of a colleague, as being "better as a writer than in getting news." But he also won praise for his coverage of a horrible train wreck and of a lynching. It was from these experiences as a reporter, he later wrote, that he began to "misdoubt the motives, professed or secret," of any man, and in pumping a source for a story, learned "to appear wise when you were ignorant, dull when you were not, disinterested when you were interested, brutal or severe when you might be just the reverse." These techniques "were the essential tricks of the trade," he concluded. Even as he mastered the news trade, he began to feel its distortions and limitations, and he turned his hand to fiction, where the problem of responsibility to his subject was quite different.

One of Dreiser's first short stories, "Nigger Jeff" (1899)—a kind of farewell to the life of reporting the "news"—describes a callow reporter sent South to cover the story of the rape of a white woman by a black man:

> Davies smiled. He was always pleased to be sent out of town.
> It was a mark of appreciation. The city editor rarely sent any
> of the other men on these big stories.

But before the tale is done Davies's smile turns to sorrow and horror as he watches the captured black man foam at the mouth while he is dragged bleeding and shuddering to his hanging. One senses Dreiser enlarging his theme beyond the possibilities of journalism; the story is a rebuke for the sort of petty pride the reporter feels before he begins to think about what he is doing.

While Dreiser's childhood had been spent in small towns where his family's shame could not be concealed, he had now made his way to an urban world where most transactions were glancing and impersonal—a shoeshine, a chain-store sale, a delivery. Such are the characteristic details of Dreiser's fictional encounters: the coin in a gentleman's pocket thrown the way of a beggar; the sexual fantasy enacted privately in the mind, as when a ticket-booth attendant follows Carrie with his eyes: " 'Good-looking,' he said to himself, and proceeded to visions of condescensions on her part which were exceedingly flattering to himself." The sense of human isolation in the city became an obsession; this was earned knowledge, confirmed by Dreiser's years as a reporter, when he discovered the city to be everywhere "latent," in Whitman's phrase, "with unseen existences."

In his memoir *Dawn*, Dreiser writes that he wished that "I were able to suggest in prose the throb and urge and sting of my first days in Chicago." In fact, he had done so thirty years before, in the opening chapters of *Sister Carrie*, with its portrait of the sublime and brutal city "open to the sweeping winds and rain . . . yet lighted throughout the night with long, blinking lines of gaslamps, fluttering in the wind." In the novel's memorable opening, Carrie Meeber, a Wisconsin farm girl, is sitting primly on a train.

She nervously watches the farmland blur beyond her window, shifting her gaze shyly to the other passengers, when, "conscious of a man behind [her] . . . observing her mass of hair . . . she felt a certain interest growing in that quarter." At first she is aware only of the sound of the man's breath and the rustle of his clothes; then he leans forward, acquiring first a face, then a name and a position—Charles Drouet, drummer for the dry-goods firm of Bartlett, Caryoe & Company.

As Drouet comes into focus, it is his clothes that define his person: a "rather tight-fitting" suit with "low crotch" vest and "linen cuffs . . . fastened with large, gold plate buttons." Later, after he has taken Carrie out of her sister's drab flat (its walls "discordantly papered . . . the floors . . . covered with matting and the hall laid with a thin rag carpet") into a bright new life as his mistress, we see him in his comfortable rooms through Carrie's wide eyes: "As he cut the meat his rings almost spoke."

When Carrie meets Hurstwood, who will replace Drouet as her lover, it is again the clothes—his stiff lapels, his mother-of-pearl buttons, and especially his shoes, which "were of soft, black calf, polished only to a dull shine"—that she chiefly notices. "Drouet wore patent leather, but Carrie could not help feeling that there was a distinction in favour of [Hurstwood's] soft leather." She has discovered the relation between status and taste.

Hurstwood's social position is precarious, however, and if Carrie does not know it he does. Left out of the real financial decisions of the saloon he manages (the power of decision being reserved by the owners, "Messrs. Fitzgerald and Moy"), he screens himself off in "a little office . . . set off in polished cherry and grill-work" from the faintly grubby job of the cashier, to whom is left the actual handling of money. In his contact with customers he has "a finely graduated scale of informality and friendship," depending on the social rank of those he is dealing with: he is easy and confidential with the low-paid clerks, quiet and deferential with the occasional well-heeled gentlemen who wander in. Within this narrow stratum—between the owners above him and the petty functionaries below—Hurstwood holds his position by his caution and charm.

On the town, he is more daring, and when he first meets Carrie, he is pleased by her lack of self-consciousness. There is nothing manipulative about her; in her "diffident manner was nothing of the art of the courtesan"; she is open and willing to be pampered and touched, "not so much calculating," as Dreiser later said of his sisters, "as vain and unthinking." Carrie's great talent, and the secret of her later success on the stage, is her "passivity of soul, which is always the mirror of the active world." She has an emotional neediness (her "mouth had the expression at times, in talking and in repose, of one who might be upon the verge of tears") that men take as a promise to be grateful for their attentions. And she is. Thanks to Drouet, "the narrow life of the country had fallen from her as a garment, and the city, with all its mystery, [had] taken its place." But Hurstwood's claim is stronger: "It was an important thing to her to hear one so well-positioned and powerful speaking" of his love for her. For Carrie, Hurstwood is more capable than Drouet of lifting her into the good life.

When she first goes onstage in an amateur theatrical Carrie's effect on the audience is exhilarating. Her hold on men like Hurstwood can be expanded to a larger audience, she senses, since the theater provides a kind of authorized voyeurism for men dulled by the routines of business and marriage. "Drouet," waiting for her after her first performance, "was palavering himself with the looseness of excitement and passion." Carrie's "body tingles" at this kind of public sexual interchange; when men praise her acting, her "eyes [turn] . . . bright, cheeks red . . . she radiated . . . pleasure." And when Hurstwood, stunned by her grace onstage, presses his advances, and gets her to leave Drouet, her feelings of guilt are as faint as her memory is short. The housemaid and neighbors mutter that she goes with other men when Drouet (whom they take to be her husband) is out of town, but "she gave little thought" to him, "thinking only of the dignity and grace of her [new] lover and of his consuming affection for her."

Carrie's fate—as the mistress first of Drouet, then of Hurstwood, then, when she has become a successful actress, of the public—has been set in motion in the subtle opening chapter by her failure to understand a basic principle of the human marketplace: that a woman does not look a strange man steadily in the eye without signaling to him that she is ready to be included in the system of exchange.

This initial failure of social understanding is also an immigrant's failure. But Carrie learns quickly. She has left home; her sister and brother-in-law cannot afford to keep her in their flat in Chicago; and she has lost her ties with her family. Her value to others creates her identity rather than the other way around. She slips easily into whatever manner or style of dress seems to get results, shedding it when fashions change or when she moves on, for she sees that survival in the city depends on adapting. This is why she is a splendid actress: "Instinctively, she felt a desire to imitate" the women whom Drouet eyed on the street, "how they set their little feet, how they carried their chins, with what grace and sinuosity they swing their bodies." Later, after she has fled to New

York with Hurstwood, she becomes a New Yorker as Hurstwood cannot: unlike him, she is uninhibited by the past.

Other American writers had begun to write about the new casualness with which human lives meet and separate in the city. William Dean Howells had written about infidelity, alcoholism, and divorce in *A Modern Instance* (1882) and, in *A Hazard of New Fortunes* (1890), had anticipated Dreiser in his account of the violence of a streetcar strike between workers and police, whose masters are comfortably far from the scene. But, unlike Howells, Dreiser was writing without a remedial purpose, from within his own and his intimately witnessed experience. He was writing as a reporter telling two inverse stories; the story of an upwardly drifting woman and that of an ordinary man's fall.

As it proceeds, the book becomes more Hurstwood's story than Carrie's. Hurstwood finds himself obsessed with this new enchanting girl. Alone one Saturday in the office, he notices that his employer's safe has not clicked shut. There begins within him a war of instincts, and, in an astonishingly powerful scene, Dreiser shows him inspecting the pouches of money—a loyal employee checking to be sure that all is in order. Then the door of the safe accidentally closes, and Hurstwood becomes, in that instant, a desperate man grasping a chance for a new life.

What follows is a mixture of panic and elation as Hurstwood coaxes Carrie onto the Montreal train and makes his run for freedom. But it is a short and pointless dash; not long afterward he is found, and, to call off the police and the company's lawyers, he returns the unspent money. Hiding now from old acquaintances, hounded by his wife, he begins his descent.

Some of the most powerful and affecting pages of *Sister Carrie* are devoted to Hurstwood's fall. Even as he stares into the open safe, and then makes his break for freedom with Carrie on the train, he is trapped, and his ruin has begun. In describing Hurstwood's subsequent collapse (the character came into his mind, Dreiser said later, as he watched bums shuffling about and sleeping in the park across from New York's City Hall), Dreiser drew on his newspaper experience in the Chicago and St. Louis slums, and on his own down-and-out days in New York, when he watched how the mannequins and fine linens on the warm side of the department store window were posed and arranged:

> The streets were bedded with [snow]—six inches of cold, soft carpet, churned to a dirty brown by the crush of teams and the feet of men. Along Broadway men picked their way in ulsters and umbrellas. . . . In the [Bowery], crowds on cold errands shifted past dingy stores, in the deep recesses of which lights were already gleaming. There were early lights in the cable cars, whose usual clatter was reduced by the mantle about the wheels.

The images of domestic comfort—beds and carpets—are bitterly evoked here as Hurstwood makes his way through the snow to the Bowery shelter and joins a group of men who

> made no effort to go in, but shifted ruefully about, digging their hands deep in their pockets and leering at the crowd and the increasing lamps. With the minutes, increased the number. . . . There was a face in the thick of the collection which was as white as drained veal.

In the book's famous ending, Carrie, now a pampered actress, watches from her suite high in the Waldorf—much too high for her to make out that white face—as the defeated men slog below her through the snow.

Here is the real reason that *Sister Carrie* shocked its first readers—not merely its sexual candor, but its unrelenting assault on the notion that one's rise or fall has anything to do with a general economy of virtue and reward or vice and punishment. Hurstwood's unpremeditated act of embezzlement is a small moment of weakness of a small man. But in Dreiser's hands it becomes the stuff of tragedy. His genius, as Richard Poirier has remarked, involved a "fascinated surrender to the mysterious forces that in the city destroy freedom and even any consciousness of its loss."

During the writing of *Sister Carrie* Dreiser released himself from his need—expressed variously in his early interest in Social Darwinism, with its vision of a predestined order beneath the violent surface of life, later in his turn to the Episcopal Church and to the Communist Party, which promised resolution in a prophesied future—to find some pattern in the apparent randomness of human lives. The novel delivers no such rationale for its events. It describes a world that runs on sex and chance, in which the human attention span is overstretched by anything beyond today's appointments or tomorrow's assignation. Hurstwood's fall is not deserved, and Carrie is not appropriately rewarded. Their fortunes have no moral meaning; they simply happen.

Dreiser's readers could not dismiss Hurstwood as an extreme case; he had stood exactly at the middle point of the American class hierarchy and was undone by a moment of desire. When Dreiser wrote *Sister Carrie*, the boundary between the middle class and the swarming lower orders was blurring and, he makes clear, could be crossed at any moment by almost anyone—in either direction. One of Sylvia's suitors, Dreiser remembered, liked to recite a popular ballad called "Over the Hill to the Poor House." For Dreiser, the hill was neither high nor far, and he saw that for every young climber there is someone else on the way down.

Although he was initially enthusiastic about *Sister Carrie*, Dreiser's publisher, Frank Doubleday, became squeamish and limited its distribution, afraid to sponsor the story of a loose woman's public triumph. Dreiser was deeply discouraged by the book's reception; there were some favorable reviewers, but most, to one degree or another, were shocked by the novel, and Doubleday's action ensured that the royalties would be negligible. Dreiser returned to journalism and sustained himself as a magazine writer, especially for *McClure's* and *Harper's Weekly*, with a number of pieces that he eventually collected in *Twelve Men*—an investigation of a foundling home; a portrait of a labor leader; an account of a retired wrestler who ran a sanatorium (where Dreiser had been a patient) in which therapy took the form of steaming, exercising, and verbally abusing the patients until they sweated out their flabbiness of mind as well as body. Slowly Dreiser rebuilt his confidence, though there were many further bouts of depression. Once, in early 1903, he recounts a particularly "gloomy and wretched" day, on which he

attended mass at the Catholic church, . . . a spectacle which I enjoyed very much. The church was soothing, the music beautiful and the lights and candles upon the altar a spectacle to behold. I rejoiced enthusiastically in it all and came home feeling as if I were better than ever.

By the end of the decade he was able to tell his friend H. L. Mencken that "I expect to try out this book game [again] for about four or five books after which unless I am enjoying a good income from them I will quit." The book with which he renewed himself as a novelist was *Jennie Gerhardt*, a simple story that Mencken thought "the best American novel . . . [since] the lonesome but Himalayan exception of *Huckleberry Finn*." The judgment is extravagant but not absurd.

The new book had first come into Dreiser's mind within days of his father's death in 1900, and old Gerhardt, a master glassblower from Germany who never manages to get a grip on life in the New World, is clearly a portrait of John Paul Dreiser. Substituting rolled newspaper for firewood to save a few pennies, he lumbers about in idleness and bewilderment, having burned his hands in molten glass much as John Paul Dreiser himself had been injured.

For this deeply personal book Dreiser tapped his own memories of youthful awkwardness and poverty. When Jennie keeps and hides a list of difficult words that she has heard in the speech of her better-bred lover, and when she feigns a lack of appetite in order not to risk using the wrong fork in the hotel restaurant, Dreiser is re-creating the embarrassment and deprivation of his own youth. With a force unprecedented in American literature, *Jennie Gerhardt* exposes the beaten wills of people living in unrelieved exhaustion and worry, teased by the proximity of the good life. And in the portrait of Jennie herself Dreiser gives expression to what his father would have called *Sehnsucht*—an undirected

longing, the unbearable sense of youth taunted by hope, then
defeated.

At first, Dreiser called his new novel (which he worked on for
nearly a decade) *The Transgressor*. It was the story of a beautiful
girl both cared for and deceived by the higher-caste men who first
lust for her, then love her, then find themselves called back to
the obligations of their class, to which she can never belong. It
is, in some respects, a reprise of Carrie's story, but this time there
is no public rise at the expense of disposable lovers. Dreiser's
sisters had lived this story (Mame and Sylvia had both given birth
to illegitimate children, one stillborn, the other given away), and
it was becoming a common tale among newly mobile Americans—
the story of the female innocent led astray by the big city, the
literary version of what was soon to become a stock subject of the
movies. But it had never been written like this: from within the
mind of the dazzled girl herself, by a writer who traced without
moralism or sentimentality the surge of pleasure and hope she
feels in the involuntary power of her body to release her from the
grim world into which she had been born.

The novel begins as a conventional cautionary tale. Jennie,
working as a hotel maid, goes door to door offering her services
as a laundress; she is seduced by a hotel guest who is no less than
a United States senator. He dies; she has his child. The terms
have been set for a story of ruin and chastisement.

Much of the book promises to deliver exactly this sort of ad-
monitory moral, as if in compensation for *Sister Carrie*, but it
becomes something entirely different. After her affair with the
senator Jennie is thrown out of the house by her father, and,
concealing her past, she drifts into the domestic employ of a
Cleveland matron, just as Dreiser's sister Sylvia, pregnant, had

been sent off to New York. There Jennie is noticed by a house-guest, Lester Kane, an "essentially animal man," who grows excited by her resistance: "Her hesitancy, her repeated protests, her gentle 'no, no, no' moved him as music might."

Lester Kane, the son of a well-established Cincinnati manufacturer, is not interested in money the way his father and brother are. He even has a touch of contempt for the business class and, consequently, for himself. We see him first as one of Dreiser's enviable sexual experts, a "strong, hairy, axiomatic" man who dispenses with all the formalities in his initial approach to Jennie: "Look here," he says, ". . . You and I might as well understand each other right now. I like you." Kane, though "born a Catholic . . . was no longer a believer in the divine inspiration of Catholicism"; he "wanted the comfort of feminine companionship, but . . . was more and more disinclined to give up his personal liberty in order to obtain it."

Lester has the characteristics of a brute: he talks patronizingly to Jennie about his plans to make her his mistress: "I'll do anything to make it easy for you." Afterward he buys her clothes so that she will turn the eyes of other men and make them envy him. But his brutality is never consummated, to use the verb that Dreiser applies to both sexual relations and business deals. When Lester discovers that Jennie has been hiding her child nearby with a paid nurse, he is furious: "He did not like to see the evidence of Jennie's previous misdeeds walking about in the shape of a human being." Though he is at first jealous and angry when he learns that his proprietorship of Jennie has not been exclusive, he nevertheless finds himself strangely softened. This feeling competes with his irritation at losing the comfort of an unencumbered mistress. As for Jennie, she is full of apology, afraid to ask or even to wonder if he might extend his affection to her child. The keener-minded Kanes intervene, the prospects of costly scandal grow, and Kane backs away, justifying his behavior by telling himself that he has suffered injury and deceit. He marries a woman of his own class and leaves Jennie with an allowance and a flat.

The chastening moral has been prepared for; when Lester pays anonymously for Jennie's father to live in a decent house, the old man experiences a physical fear at the prospect of living among fine and fragile things: "It's so easy," he says, "to scratch things up, and then it's all over." In *Jennie Gerhardt* the rule of the marketplace applies: used goods do not hold their price.

But Dreiser yearns for a world where this rule can be suspended. The intransigent Gerhardt forgives Jennie for the sin of having had an illegitimate child, after he has taken his granddaughter to be baptized and has "brooded on the words and the duties [of] the sacrament." When Dreiser describes how the old man, watching the child asleep on the white counterpane in her cradle, "received a light," he seems much closer to the spirit of Old World Catholicism than to the cruel culture of the New World that Carrie has learned to exploit. Jennie remains an alien in this merciless Protestant culture, where the experience of failure—whether moral or material—is articulated as spiritual transgression. Why, Dreiser has her wonder after her "fall," were the hotel guests always chucking her under the chin and proposing more than talk? "Could it be because there was something innately bad about her, an inward corruption that attracted its like?" Hurstwood was Dreiser's embodiment of the human waste in American life, a man whom we cannot quite honor or condemn, an American schooled in self-reliance and (when hard times come) in self-hatred. Though he has moments of anger toward

Carrie and others, he blames his fall squarely on himself, judging that "the game is up" and lost. As Jennie begins to think like him, we can feel Dreiser's rising pity.

Jennie is a failed Carrie; she goes nowhere on the promise of her beauty. But in another sense Dreiser redeems her: when Kane is dying, after he has been blackmailed by his family into leaving Jennie and making a respectable marriage, she returns—a figure in whom the grieving Virgin and Mary Magdalene are conflated—to his bedside, an exceptional and moving moment in Dreiser because it is a transaction in which the only medium of exchange is love. With his shrewish wife and sister offstage, Kane, who, like most of Dreiser's characters, has meager experience with the spoken word as a conveyor of emotion, manages to say: "I've always wanted to say to you, Jennie, that I haven't been satisfied with the way we parted. . . . I loved you, I love you. I want to tell you that." Here Dreiser has written, and revised, the bitter lives of his sisters.

After Kane's death, Jennie enters a Catholic church for the first time, and, in a scene that Saul Bellow may have had in mind for Tommy Wilhelm's final dissolution in *Seize the Day* (1956), she sits hidden from the other mourners in a back pew at the funeral:

> There were the chanted invocations and responses, the sprinkling of the coffin with holy water, the lighting and swinging of the censer and then the mumbled responses of the auditors to the Lord's Prayer and to its Catholic addition, the invocation to the Blessed Virgin. . . . To Jennie the candles, the incense, the holy song were beautiful. . . . She was as a house filled with mournful melody and the presence of death. She cried and cried.

Some fifty years earlier Nathaniel Hawthorne had described the adulteress Hester Prynne walking in shame through a crowd of merciless New England Puritans. "Had there been a Papist among the crowd," Hawthorne wrote, "he might have seen in this beautiful woman . . . an object to remind him of the image of Divine Maternity." Jennie is driven from the church when she reveals herself. It was as a witness to this expulsion that Dreiser rendered modern American life in prose so compassionate that it reaches the intensity of religious devotion.

9

What Would Edith Wharton Think?

When Edith Wharton supervised the design of her summer house at Lenox, Massachusetts, she made it, inside and out, a showcase of propriety. Facing the house (which she called The Mount, after her grandfather's estate), one finds a rhythm of windows and doors that is absolutely regular, though closer inspection reveals that several of the front "windows" are illusions created by closed shutters. When one looks through a real window and sees what appears to be another window opening onto the rear garden, it turns out to be a mirror placed on an interior wall. Inside, every room is relentlessly symmetrical; if a door is hung off-center, you can count on its being balanced by a second door on the same wall even if this one opens onto nothing but a solid panel. And if a room is meant to feel enclosed and tranquil yet needs access to the adjacent room, a knobless door is disguised by continuous molding and blends in imperceptibly with the wall.

This world seems utterly false to us. Where we value candor, Wharton valued tact. A perfect expression of her aesthetic imagination, The Mount is a treasury of trompes l'oeil, in which deception and concealment are turned to the service of surface harmonies. It is the house of a woman who, though contemptuous of the saturated Victorian interiors in which she had grown up, had not yet made the turn toward the modern. And her principles of design were not far from her literary practice: where we esteem writing that probes and discloses, she still wrote about surfaces in a prose whose sibilance and alliteration evoke the swish and glitter of the dance:

> the light of the wax candles fell on revolving tulle skirts, on girlish heads wreathed with modest blossoms, on the dashing aigrettes and ornaments of the young married women's coiffures, and on the glitter of highly glazed shirtfronts and fresh glacé gloves.

The chief decoration of Wharton's houses—their women—are dressed according to the same principles of containment and concealment. Laced and corseted, they display neck and shoulders but not much else. If a hint of sexual frankness comes through these prescribed limits, it is judged "perverse and provocative," as in the case of the Countess Olenska's "long robe of red velvet [that was] bordered about the chin and down the front with glossy black fur"—a properly opaque wrapping that leaves every man atremble with the thought of the skin and hair it conceals and emulates.

Edith Wharton had grown up in a "hieroglyphic world where the real thing is never said or done or even thought," and life was conducted in "an atmosphere of faint implications and pale delicacies." She belonged to a class in which a scandalous affair would be manifest in the way a married man sits slouched in a chair while a woman who is not his wife stands beside him (as her friend and mentor Henry James conveys the fact of adultery in *The Portrait of a Lady*), or (in *The Ambassadors*) in the way a man and woman sit together in a rowboat, he in his shirtsleeves.

We tend to consider this superseded world as prudish and unfree. We think of its people as imprisoned. And yet we are drawn to it powerfully, as to an object of desire. The Manhattan audience with whom I stood on line to see Martin Scorsese's 1993 film of *The Age of Innocence* (Wharton's best novel, published in 1920, when she was nearly sixty) was, according to the standards of her time and class, a band of degenerates. Some couples were sexually demonstrative. Others (it was a sticky evening) wore clothing more revealing than concealing and spoke what Wharton would have regarded as gutter talk. When the audience got inside and the film got rolling, however, there were only noises of contentment. The theater sounded as if it were filled with kids humming while eating chocolate. Scorsese's slow pans over dining tables laden with Japanese and Meissen porcelain, arrangements of camellias and lilies, incised silver and decanted wine, were greeted with audible sighs and murmurs.

These are the sort of people who are loyal to *Masterpiece Theatre*, Laura Ashley, Merchant and Ivory, the Bombay Company, and Victoria's Secret. They are, presumably, the people whom Bloomingdale's and Columbia Pictures had in mind for their movie tie-in offer of a $1,000 gift certificate for the best "100-word true or fictional story" about unfulfilled love. (For second-prize winners, they promised to send two dozen yellow roses to "someone you loved," the romance being all in the verb's past tense.) During the film's first run, I woke up every morning to a radio announcement that Scorsese's movie was supporting *Morn-*

ing Edition, the compleat yuppie's favorite source of news and opinion, and the same spot ran in the afternoons on *All Things Considered*.

What was going on? Why do so many of us who live in the age of explicitness, when a man in Newland Archer's position would surely run off with his Countess, seem to yearn for the age of discretion? The Wharton revival—a new edition of her unfinished novel *The Buccaneers* was a Book-of-the-Month Club main selection while *The Age of Innocence* packed the houses—contains a hint of an answer, I think. This was not an isolated phenomenon. Recently a "sequel" has been written of Jane Austen's *Pride and Prejudice*, from which readers can learn whether Elizabeth and Darcy kept the fires glowing. The cover story of an issue of *Psychology Today* was entitled "Rekindling Old Flames." And Scorsese, the director of such gritty movies as *GoodFellas*, *Raging Bull*, and *Mean Streets*, is blunt about what drew him to Wharton's drawing rooms and gardens and botanical pavilions: before, he says, he "never really found the right thing for romance, because . . . I don't *know* it in the modern world. I can't sense it . . . so therefore I . . . want[ed] to do something very lush and sensual from a period where the texture was stronger."

Scorsese's film succeeds because it catches the feeling of a time when conflict between public propriety and private desire was an inescapable fact of life, and when, if they came into direct opposition, the former proved stronger than the latter. It is about a social order that put a price on illicit pleasure, and it returns us to a virtually medieval idea of chaste love. In the central scene where the Countess (still married to her Polish rogue of a husband and inhibited from seeking a divorce because he has threatened to publicize her own infidelities) tells Archer that she can only love him by giving him up, Scorsese conveys the exquisite pain of obstructed desire by turning the two of them into a human arabesque. They coil together, tortured, until their clothed bodies make one continuous sinew—his head arched down to her hip, hers thrown forward upon the curve of his back, a brilliant visual emblem for the passion to which they cannot submit. No less than Francis Ford Coppola's blood-drenched *Dracula* (a film more obviously informed by the presence of AIDS as the chief symbol of mortality in contemporary consciousness), this is also a work about salvation through renunciation. The only removal of clothes comes in an intensely erotic scene when Archer, pressed close against Ellen in a narrow brougham, unbuttons and peels back her tight calfskin gloves and kisses her exposed wrists.

That Scorsese managed to make a sexy movie with a PG rating was no small triumph in this age of explicitness, since there is always a compulsion (and a commercial reward) for exceeding the frankness of last year. Scorsese seems to have realized that the steady intensification of the erotic currency in our culture—more violence, more raunch, more speed—has led to a certain depreciation of it. And so, with a charming haughtiness, he reversed course and made a film about a world that insisted on standing still. He touched a nerve because his film reminds us that in such a world—where conventional kisses tended to be "a fugitive pressure on [the] lips" or a brush of "the forehead with the tip of his moustache"—the possibilities for real passion may have been incomparably larger than in our own.

Edith Wharton reported on a small privileged corner of this world with precision and elegance. Her portraits of women without beauty or wealth are studies in the experience of being discarded, and the figure of Ellen Olenska in *The Age of Innocence* only hints at the lifelong torture to which unhappily married women were condemned. She wrote with a combination of sympathy and disgust about women who used their sexuality, with trained calculation, to preserve or build their social station, and about the men who used them to breed. Here, from *The Custom of the Country* (1913), is the icy Undine Spragg issuing her first kiss:

> It was the first time she had permitted [her suitor] a kiss, and as his face darkened down on her she felt a moment's recoil. But her physical reactions were never very acute: she always vaguely wondered why people made "such a fuss," were so violently for or against such demonstrations. A cool spirit within her seemed to watch over and regulate her sensations, and leave her capable of measuring the intensity of those she provoked.

Wharton could write this way because, despite her charter membership in this world, in certain moods she hated it. She described the old New York crowd as "aborigines" when the pejorative force of that word was still unqualified. She herself lived half in it and half out. She took a lover in her forties, long before she terminated her own sexless marriage by divorce. She stood with Newland Archer when he protests that he and his peers were "as like each other as those dolls cut out of the same folded paper . . . like patterns stencilled on a wall." And she wrote with disgust about the "vacant serenity" of Archer's "limpid" bride, May Welland, and about his sister, Janey, whose "brown and purple poplins hung, as the years went on, more and more slackly on her virgin frame." Wharton loathed these deracinated people, and set them up in *The Age of Innocence* like a ring of mannequins surrounding the two living beings—Archer and the Countess—whom she placed at the book's center.

Yet at the root of Wharton's art is the fact that she could not do without this orderly world and was unwilling, like the Countess Olenska, to give it up. Since R. W. B. Lewis's biography was published in 1975, it has been known that Wharton had been carrying on for years a passionate extramarital affair with a man of the world named Morton Fullerton. We also know that she composed some remarkably free-spirited pornography (which the scholar Cynthia Griffin Wolff has dated around 1918). In some respects, then, *The Age of Innocence* is a retelling of Wharton's own story, but with the sexual release deferred. Its hampered lovers are denied their consummation even though Wharton clearly *felt*, when the Countess first taps Archer's "knee with her plumed fan," how this mediated touch "thrills him like a caress." She denied them because she also knew how this explosive moment threatened to blow apart the world he is reluctant to renounce and into which the Countess wishes to be admitted.

If it is today almost impossible to apprehend the conditions under which men and women once felt morally tested by such a choice between desire and respectability, it had already become a challenge for Wharton in 1920. By then she was speaking of the nineteenth century as "a blessed refuge from the turmoil and mediocrity of today," and knew she had written a book about what she later called that "distant period of the 70s," which seemed, with "every year that passes . . . more like a fairy tale." She wanted her novel to be taken not as a "costume drama" but as a "simple

and grave" story about "two people trying to live up to something"—a code of social propriety—"that was still 'felt in the
blood.' "

Wharton was devoted to this disappearing culture (as a subject
and, in some moods, as an ideal) because it had been built, above
all, on the principle of tact, on the central recognition that once
a transgressive impulse is expressed or publicly acted upon, it can
never be retracted. There is no such thing, this culture knew, as
a jury that can truly "disregard" something it has heard or seen,
no matter how sternly instructed by the judge. Once you have
strayed, you are branded an outsider. This is a world without
forgiveness. Thus there is a gangsterish quality to Wharton's old
New York social clique, which, when someone steps out of line,
proves as expert at shunning, expulsion, and other forms of social
murder as any of Scorsese's mobsters. Scorsese's previous work
prepared him well for translating the late scenes of this novel in
which the family musters its force to expel the Countess and then
links arms to keep her out lest she return to carry off one of its
sons.

We have a name for writers who chronicle the lives of such
people: we call them "novelists of manners." Yet surely this phrase
is a tautology. All novels are ultimately about the predicament of
the self as it is contained within some social structure—that is to
say, within some system of rules. The learning of manners, the
hatred of them and yet the relief at their compulsion, their cruelty
to the self and yet their necessity for social coherence, has been
the stuff of fiction from the start. The novel is a literary form that
can exist only as long as something like balance persists between
the inhibiting influence of social authority and the insolence of
the individual. For this reason, the form has been deranged lately

by the loss of the concept of legitimate inhibition, indeed the legitimacy of culture itself. Wharton did have an impulse to pull off the tablecloth and send everything crashing to the floor. She was a bohemian. She was a feminist. But she was first and foremost a novelist, and she knew that without manners there can be no stories.

This dividedness is the quality that gives *The Age of Innocence* its tautness and intimacy, and makes it Wharton's best book. In its famous closing scene, the now widowed Newland Archer sits rooted to a bench in a Paris square beneath the windows of Ellen's apartment, to which his son has led him in the hope of allowing his father a reunion with the woman whom, the son now knows, he had loved far beyond his dutiful feelings toward his mother. Archer gazes up at the flat, imagines the figure of the woman he loved and relinquished, and says quietly to himself, "It's more real to me here than if I went up." Then he gets up and walks back to his hotel alone. In this phrase and act, all the force of Wharton's art and thought is summed up. Though Scorsese makes mistakes along the way (the music is too sinister; Daniel Day-Lewis's Archer is, at first, too dusky; Michelle Pfeiffer cannot quite convey such subtleties as a "smile [passing] from [Ellen's] eyes to her lips"), he has remained loyal to the spirit of Wharton's painful book.

Nothing, unfortunately, could be less true of another popular Wharton event that same season—the appearance of a new version, "completed" by Marion Mainwaring, of *The Buccaneers*, Wharton's final and unfinished novel. *The Buccaneers* is an interesting book in Wharton's career, not just because it was the last (she began work on it in the early 1930s, and she worked on it sporadically until her death in 1937) but also because in it she returns to the historical moment that had captivated her in *The Age of Innocence*, when the rules of high social life had been stable and clear. The work of an old woman writing fancifully about the young, it was written at the close of Wharton's years as a grande dame, when she held court at her suburban Paris estate to intellectuals with advanced ideas. It came after her reading in Nietzsche and Proust and Freud and Dreiser, and after her friendships with Sinclair Lewis and Aldous Huxley and her encounters with Scott Fitzgerald. It would seem to be the work of a woman who has broken free of the constraints that had hemmed in her peers in the age of innocence.

And its story promises to conform to such expectations. It is the tale of two dashing daughters whose father's money is too "new" to gain them acceptance in New York society. Since English gentlemen, in need of fresh fortunes to keep up their estates, have fewer scruples about the pedigrees of their brides, the girls are sent to take their chances in England. The result for the older one, the conventional beauty, is a marriage that improves her social station. For the younger one, Annabel (Nan), who is a vivacious seeker, the result is a marriage to the tradition-bound Duke of Tintagel, who soon disappoints her both spiritually and sexually and from whom she drifts away toward a dreamy young gentleman portentously named Guy.

This plot promises not just a revisiting of *The Age of Innocence* but a revision of it—or so, at least, Marion Mainwaring wants it to be. Wharton did leave a sketchy "scenario" of an ending which indicates that she intended her heroine to leave her husband and join her lover, and she had completed twenty-nine chapters which are inconclusive in respect to the unwritten denouement. Mainwaring is determined to make the story come out right this time. And so she not only "completes" the ending but intervenes in places that Wharton herself had completed. She plants very broad hints in the middle of Wharton's narrative—inventing, for instance, a speech by the Duke on his taste in collecting ("there is no satisfaction," Mainwaring has him say, "in owning a fragment") that prepares the way for his remarriage after Nan has left him. He will end up, Mainwaring hints heavily, with a rich widow whose late husband just happened to have owned the other half of a classical sculpture whose fragment belongs to the Duke.

A little of this sort of thing goes a long way. But Mainwaring never loses her nerve for freely supplementing Wharton's dialogue, though Wharton herself, in her memoir *A Backward Glance* (1933), said that dialogue was "an effect to be sparingly used." She even subjects Wharton's text to a politically correct cleansing, making silent expurgations throughout that she justifies by the tiresome explanation that "changes have been made . . . when . . . Wharton referred to race in terms offensive to modern readers." Perhaps some enterprising editor should go back to *The House of Mirth* (1905) and expunge the lines about the "small, stock-taking eyes" of the Jewish businessman, Rosedale. The political corrector's work is never done.

Even less explicable are Mainwaring's putative stylistic improvements, which are also unsignaled. Wharton, for instance, reports her heroine's discovery that she has married a sexless man by writing: "The thought that she had even imagined Ushant [the Duke] as a lover made her smile, and she turned away from the window." Mainwaring distends this sentence by inserting a phrase with which she can flog the poor Duke for his prudery and make sure that the obtuse reader gets the point: "The thought that she had even imagined Ushant as a lover—imagined him, any more than his mother, *approving* of pleasure—made Annabel smile, and she turned away from the window." These silent emendations are injected here and there without brackets or footnotes, nothing more than a remark in a one-paragraph afterword that "the passages I have interpolated in the original text serve to reconcile discrepancies in the narrative or prepare for later developments."

My point here is not that one should make a sacred object out of Wharton's text. Scorsese, after all, also fiddles with it. When Archer, for instance, speaks in the novel of "harlots," Scorsese has the actor speak of "whores." When in the novel Archer first touches the Countess and is engulfed by the sheer power of her physical presence, Wharton conveys this sensation by writing that "far down the inverted telescope he saw the pale white figure of [his betrothed] May Welland," while Scorsese breaks up the image and relocates it in a scene where we see May small and inverted through the lens of the bridal photographer. In another scene that has no exact corollary in the novel, he leaches out her image completely by washing the screen with a burst of orange-red light into which she disappears as if incinerated. These are acts of genuine translation from one genre to another. But what in the world does Mainwaring think she is doing when she effects her "improvements" in a written text that still bears Wharton's name?

The Buccaneers was no masterpiece, but Mainwaring's tampering raises the question of whether we have reached the point in our attitude toward artistic integrity when we would applaud, say, the improver of the old masters who walked into the National Gallery in London and started to color in Leonardo's cartoon?

Mainwaring is apparently devoted to Wharton, but in fact she has only provided another warning about the damage that devotion can do. Perhaps she arrived at her changes through a careful study of manuscript variants (several versions survive in the Beinecke Library at Yale), but then she should have said so. More likely, what we have here is a case of presumptuous tinkering. As it stands, this edition of *The Buccaneers* is a pastiche—the larger part composed by a writer devoted to precision and rhetorical tact, the smaller part by a writer whose ear is uncertain and who cannot leave the original work alone.

It should be noted that the first published version of *The Buccaneers* was already an act of collaboration, since it was established by Wharton's executor, Gaillard Lapsley (who explained that it was simply "too good to hold back"), from manuscripts that Wharton left in various states of incomplete revision. But the responsible thing to do, which is exactly what Viola Hopkins Winner has done in her annotated edition (published by the University Press of Virginia), which reprints *The Buccaneers* along with a novel that Wharton wrote in her teens, *Fast and Loose*, is to try to get the text as close to Wharton's final intention as possible, and to indicate where surmise and editorial choice are at work.

A further trouble with Mainwaring's interventions is that the distance between the two writers is painfully large. From one of Wharton's matrons we get this marvelous evaluation of the older sister: "She will probably get whatever she wants in life, and will give in return only her beautiful profile. I don't believe her soul has a full face." From Mainwaring we get Nan putting "her hand to her heart as if she had been stabbed" when she hears that Guy is being urged toward another woman, and then a long passage where it is not clear whether she is contemplating an atlas or a globe, until we are told that "as the countries of the world rolled past in varnished yellows, pale greens, and pinks . . . the small world that was herself was suddenly decentralized." Decentralized? The word is as appropriate as a saxophone in a classical string quartet.

The list of stylistic offenses can go on, but the bad fit between the body of the text and Mainwaring's concluding chapters is also thematic. Wharton was a writer who believed that "a frivolous society can acquire dramatic significance only through what its frivolity destroys" and that the "tragic implication" of such frivolity "lies in its power of debasing people and ideals." Yet Mainwaring prepares with callow eagerness for the final act of Nan's abandoning her husband, which Wharton had indicated in her "scenario," until it becomes not just the central drama of the book but its required culmination. In fact, the scenario, as well as a long passage in *A Backward Glance*, suggests that Wharton was more deeply interested in the psychological consequences of these events for another character, Nan's governess, who has urged her on toward freedom, and that the elopement itself is almost subsidiary.

In Mainwaring's version, the escape from marriage becomes the sole point: First Nan reads, in various fictions, about tyrannical and sexually cold husbands. Then she daydreams about the time, as a child, when she and her sister, "to their mother's horror . . . had tucked up their pinafores and ridden a broad-backed Shetland pony astride." After a sufficient dose of such reading and remembering, Mainwaring figures that Nan is hot enough for her rendezvous with her lover—but we, the readers, are simply embarrassed by all the foreplay. Wharton's book, in sum, has been transformed into a bodice ripper, complete with the appearance of the conquering hero mounted "on a roan mare" and looking so dashing that Nan's "heart seemed to turn over inside her, and her hands on the reins became tight fists as she halted." Guy "mutter[s] against her cheek"; she strokes his "thick fair hair," and as she shivers at "every breath of the body so close to hers," he tells her that she is "like a flower unfolding . . . a rose coming to bloom." All this panting and crooning is a far cry from the bittersweet restraint with which Wharton herself writes about the coming together of socially unsanctioned lovers in her late novels such as *Hudson River Bracketed* (1929) and *The Gods Arrive* (1932), in which she has them sit silent, with at most a touch of hands, or a pensive walk together arm in arm.

Some years ago, in an essay that became famous, Barbara Probst Solomon wrote (after Scribner's had released its doctored version of Hemingway's last novel, *The Garden of Eden*) that "nobody can finish an unfinished novel for a writer, and nobody should presume to try." Of course, it has been done before—with Dickens's *The Mystery of Edwin Drood* and Stephen Crane's *The O'Ruddy*—and it will be done again. But there is something particularly troubling about this case.

What Mainwaring has done is to drag Edith Wharton into our time, by turning her novel into a triumphant story of a young woman's escape from a passionless marriage. But there is reason to doubt that Wharton would have written it with anything like Mainwaring's jolly insouciance. The dissolution of Wharton's own marriage caused her pain and self-doubt, and her sexual awakening with Fullerton was psychologically very complex. Moreover, there is even greater reason to doubt whether Wharton would have written it at all. Mainwaring's premise seems to be that this novel was left unfinished for the simple reason that its author died. She has made a spectacular mistake.

For there is evidence that Wharton was struggling in her waning months with what she had written. As Viola Winner says in a textual note to the annotated edition, she "devoted her creative energy . . . to revision of what . . . was the first three-fourths of the book rather than forging ahead to complete it." One of her friends, to whom she had shown the work, "counted five sets of revisions." Every writer knows that continual revision can be a delaying tactic when the will to plunge ahead is lacking, and though I do not presume to know the reason why this will was slackening for Edith Wharton, it is at least possible, it seems to me, that she did not finish *The Buccaneers* not because of failing health but because she was not fully committed to carrying out the ending which her own "scenario" prescribed.

The Buccaneers constitutes one of those instances in American literary history—along with Twain's *Huckleberry Finn* and Howells's *A Hazard of New Fortunes*—where the text itself suggests a blockage in the mind of the writer, an impediment to completion. Its most deeply felt pages are not about release and the allure of freedom but about resignation and the imperatives of duty.

Here is Nan midway in the novel as she begins to ponder her fate:

Here [in England] . . . everything was done by rule, and according to tradition, and for the Duchess of Tintagel to keep her guests waiting for luncheon would have been an offence against conventions almost as great as that of not being at her post when the company were leaving the night before. A year ago [she] would have laughed at these rules and observances; now, though they chafed her no less, she was beginning to see the use of having one's whims and one's rages submitted to some kind of control. . . .

Yes; in spite of her anger, in spite of her desperate sense of being trapped, Annabel felt in a confused way that the business of living was perhaps conducted more wisely at Longlands . . .

This is the authentic Wharton, the writer who despised the constraints imposed upon the spirit of a vibrant young woman but who also wrote with feeling about the drudgery and toil of the stoic men who supplied such women with daily flowers with which to adorn themselves. It is the Wharton who imagined real human freedom only in what she called "the republic of spirit," and who wrote not only about the pain of entrapment but about the possibilities of dignity for the trapped. And here is Archer thinking back on his life with May:

Their long years together had shown him that it did not so much matter if marriage was a dull duty, as long as it kept the dignity of a duty: lapsing from that, it became a mere battle of ugly appetites. Looking about him, he honored his own past and mourned for it. After all, there was good in the old ways.

Edith Wharton was much too serious an artist to have brought *The Buccaneers* to a banal ending. The worst mutilation in Mainwaring's edition is the fact that she finished *The Buccaneers* at all.

10

The New *Native Son*

first read *Native Son* in unreflective fascination when I was sixteen. I remember feeling queasy during the early scenes when the bubbly Chicago heiress Mary Dalton and her fast-talking radical boyfriend patronize a ghetto boy and conscript him as a tour guide for a cruise through the "black belt." Reading these scenes made me think of the time in grade school when I had invited a black child from the "projects" to my suburban home. After introducing him to my mother, I waited for him to join us for lunch, until his plate of ravioli had grown cold and I discovered that he had climbed out the window of our first-floor bathroom and run back down the hill to school. For nearly ten years I had not begun to imagine the mental storm that must have sent him out that window—until I read of Bigger's panic over whether to enter the Daltons' house through the front door or back, of his shrinking when the white housemaid approaches so close that he can "see a tiny mole at the corner of her mouth," and of his "misjudging how far back he was sitting" in an over-plump chair, so that, "conscious of every square inch of skin on his black body," he has to struggle to his feet when the "amused" Mr. Dalton arrives to interview him for the job of chauffeur. These passages made me retrospectively embarrassed and confused.

When I next read *Native Son*, I was living near Boston, and it delivered a different shock of recognition. It compelled me to move in memory between the scenes where Dalton's private detective, trying to scare the truth out of Bigger about Mary's disappearance, calls him a "*goddamn* black sonofabitch!" and a sunny afternoon at Fenway Park, when, sitting for once in a really good box seat, I had found myself behind a pair of plaid-slacked fans who spent the whole game heckling the Red Sox first baseman for being a "black bastard" in a voice loud enough for him to hear.

And now that I have read *Native Son* again, this time with a mind clogged by other books, I find myself in the grip of an entirely new experience. This is partly because Arnold Rampersad and the editors of the Library of America have given us not the original published version of 1940, but the text of the bound galleys that lay, for weeks during the fall of 1939, on the submission desk at the Book-of-the-Month Club, while the directors fretted over whether they could tolerate Bigger masturbating in a movie theater or Mary Dalton moving her "hips . . . in a hard and veritable grind" against his black body. Richard Wright was a young writer tasting his first chance for fame, and so when the verdict came in that these scenes had to be cut if the book club was to select his novel, he agreed. At last, with the deletions now restored, we have, as Rampersad says, the words of the book as Wright "wanted them to be read."

It is always a tricky business to disqualify a text that a living author has at least tacitly approved. A few years ago a group of scholars, working on the premise that Dreiser had been bullied into making changes in the text of *Sister Carrie* just before it went to press, put forward a new text based on his typescript, and the Library of America wisely refrained from following suit. This time the Library has rejected the text in which an American classic has been known for half a century. The publication of this new edition is therefore not just an editorial innovation but a major event in American literary history.

There can be no doubt that the book is better for the restorations. For one thing, the restored text solves some consistency problems, as when the State's Attorney tells Bigger, "I knew about that dirty trick you and your friend Jack pulled off in the Regal Theatre"—a statement that floats without antecedent in the 1940 text but, in the intact version, refers to Bigger's "polishing his night stick" in the movie house. More important than such textual repairs is their total effect: we now have the first book in American literary history that represents the full, urgent sexuality of a young black man. Here he moves upon Bessie's body, with whom he lies among the garbage and rats in an abandoned tenement where they are hiding from the vigilantes and police:

> The loud demand of the tensity of his own body was a voice that drowned out hers. In the cold darkness of the room it seemed that he was on some vast turning wheel that made him want to turn faster and faster; that in turning faster he would get warmth and sleep and be rid of his tense fatigue. He was conscious of nothing now but her and what he

wanted. He flung the cover back, ignoring the cold, and not knowing that he did it. . . . His desire was naked and hot in his hand and his fingers were touching her. . . . He heard her breathing heavily and heard his own breath going and coming heavily. *Bigger.* Now. All. All. Now. All. *Bigger* . . .

He lay still, feeling rid of that hunger and tenseness and hearing the wail of the night wind over and above his and her breathing. He turned from her and lay on his back again, stretching his legs wide apart.

Native Son is a book about the imperatives of the body—about Bigger's panic-sweat beading on his skin; about his convulsive stomach pain when he gulps water after parched days on the run; about his struggle to will his erection to subside while a white woman and man have sex on the car seat behind him. There are brilliant descriptions of Bigger forcing a street crony to lick the blade of his knife in an act of public submission, and of his chewing frantically his first loaf of bread in days, until it bulges his cheeks like a trumpeter's and coaxes the scarce saliva from his tongue.

The book has an almost brutal immediacy, which the newly restored text not only confirms but heightens. I have never been able to drive past the severe houses of Hyde Park or through the tangent black neighborhoods without seeing Bigger huddled against a steamed window in a passing streetcar, or seeing the snow fall softly, as if flake by flake, onto the Daltons' blue Buick that he has left parked in their gated driveway. One feels pushed by the wind off the lake toward the edge of the plains; one peers with Bigger through the "gauzelike curtain of snow" at the streetlights that taunt him with the promise of warmth—"street lamps covered with thick coatings of snow, gleaming like huge frosted moons above his head."

For Dreiser forty years earlier (from whose *An American Tragedy* Wright may have gotten the idea of a half-conscious murder), these lamps had been "blinking lines of gas-lamps, fluttering in the wind," but they were already Chicago's visual signature—tiny fires disappearing in long perspectival lines that lead out of the city into the prairie distance. Like Dreiser, Wright was not a native-born Chicagoan; his early years in Mississippi are the subject of *Black Boy* (1945), the book in which he recounted his awakening from a brutal childhood. The son of an illiterate sharecropper who deserted the family, Wright struggled against poverty and the intransigent reality of Southern racism. He was bounced from grandmother to aunt to orphanage while his mother sank into invalidism and despair. His brilliance and his discontent began to find literary expression during his schooling in Memphis, and, at nineteen, he moved to the great Midwestern city, where he quickly became, in his guts, a Chicago writer. Wright was aware, as New England and Southern and even New York writers were less likely to be early in this century, that all class distinctions in America were of absurdly recent vintage, and vulnerable to a surge or drop in the commodity market or to the perpetual real estate scramble. Wright was a student of both the dreamless poor and the cocksure rich, whom he found locked in vicious interdependence in Chicago.

Though he broke with the Communist Party in 1937, he did not leave the national party until 1942 and was still trying to construct *Native Son* within the framework of a class analysis. He had been active in the 1930s in the John Reed Club, a largely white literary organization sponsored by the Communists, and later became Harlem editor of *The Daily Worker*. His early novel *Lawd Today!* (published posthumously) is largely an evocation of soul-deadening labor; its central character, like Wright himself (who held jobs during these years as a ditchdigger, delivery boy, dishwasher, hospital worker), is a postal clerk whose body becomes a mechanical extension of the canceling machine and whose mind can only accommodate "images [that] would flit [in] . . . and then aimlessly out again, like stray cats." The early stories, collected in *Uncle Tom's Children* (1938), look back to the South, and are concerned with the gathering desperation of rural blacks, whose inarticulate rage against a world owned by white men was beginning to take the form of apocalyptic expectation.

This implicit Communist criticism of capitalist society is still at work in *Native Son*. Wright gives Bigger an incipient proletarian consciousness, a desire to "merge himself with others and be a part of this world, to lose himself in it so he could find himself, to be allowed a chance to live like others, even though he was black." As part of the same allegory of class conflict, Wright draws the kindly Mr. Dalton as a stock figure from agitprop fiction—a giver to causes who sends his servants to night school even as he rakes in the rent from black tenants who live five to a rat-infested room, a contradiction of which "in a sullen way Bigger was conscious." And if Dalton keeps a human screen of "house niggers" between him and the brutal reality of the plantation, he has an overseer to do his dirty work—Britten, the thick-necked security man, who studies Bigger to see if he waves his hands about and if his voice rises at the ends of sentences, clues that would clinch his theory that he has been fraternizing with Jews.

Here, under rough interrogation, Bigger begins to see the futility of his plan to blame Mary's murder on Jan, her Communist boyfriend: "Britten loosened his fingers from Bigger's collar and shrugged his shoulders. Bigger relaxed, still standing, his head resting against the wall, aching. He had not thought that anyone would dare think that he, a black Negro, would be Jan's partner." This remarkable phrase, "black Negro," is not a tautology, but a clue that the concept of "Negro" is, for Wright, not fundamentally a racial idea. "Negro" is a generic word for hopelessness and degradation. The early pages on Bigger—his portrait as a gang leader who compensates with cruelty for his sense of exile from the world of satisfactions—are almost indistinguishable in social content from James T. Farrell's portrait of the Irish thug in *Studs Lonigan* (1932–35).

But a "black Negro" is something quite different, something for which Bigger hates himself more than he hates his oppressor. A "black Negro" is worse than the refuse of the white world, he knows, since he is a creature held by whites of every class (from tycoons to vigilantes, they all close ranks in his pursuit) to be not only low and incorrigible but foul and poisonous. A wall stands between Bigger and the sensations he craves. He finds himself smacked back like a dog that lifts its head to the table rather than wait for the white man's scraps to fall to the floor. Not merely exploited, he is despised; and *Native Son*, almost in spite of itself, is a book about this distinction.

In other words, it is a book about self-hatred, about a young man who loathes his own color and physiognomy and dialect and all the features of his irreparable social ugliness. Bigger is not so much an autonomous consciousness as he is the projection of the white imagination, a figure whose closest precursors in American fiction come not from previous black writers but from racist white writers (such as Thomas Dixon, author of *The*

Clansman [1905]) for whom black men were nothing more than clothed apes. Earlier black writers had certainly remarked the "peculiar sensation," as W. E. B. Du Bois famously put it, of a "double-consciousness, this sense of always looking at one's self through the eyes of others, of measuring one's soul by the tape of a world that looks on in amused contempt and pity." But before Wright, black novelists had tended to approach this psychological dilemma from a connoisseur's distance and with Jamesian finesse, as in the tradition of the mulatto novel, which dramatized the mixed relief and guilt of light-skinned blacks who tried to solve the problem of double-consciousness by obliterating their black identity altogether.

In the 1920s and 1930s black literary intellectuals, especially those who participated in what became known as the Harlem Renaissance, turned more openly to a celebration of their African identity, a gesture with which Wright sympathized but which he suspected of self-delusion and accommodation to the prurient white taste for exoticism. Wright was working toward an unblinking confrontation with the problem of black identity in *Lawd Today!* and in the stories of *Uncle Tom's Children*. But it is in *Native Son* that he gives full voice, despite Bigger's lumpish inarticulateness, to the anguish of the "black Negro":

What did he want? What did he love and what did he hate? He did not know. There was something he *knew* and something he *felt*; something the *world* gave him and something he *himself* had; something spread out in *front* of him and something spread out in *back*; and never in all his life, with this black skin of his, had the two worlds, thought and feeling, will and mind, aspiration and satisfaction, been together;

never had he felt a sense of wholeness. . . . only under the stress of hate was the conflict resolved.

What Bigger discovers in the moments when he kills is that his reactive life of shame and fear can become hideously creative, that he can animate the ghostly world through which he has been wandering in numb fright. A cup of hot milk, a shot of whiskey, the touch of Bessie's flesh, even the very conditions of hunger and desire, become reassurances of life itself:

> The memory of the bottle of milk Bessie had heated for him last night came back so strongly that he could almost taste it. . . . He saw himself take the top off the white bottle, with some of the warm milk spilling over his black fingers, and then lift the bottle to his mouth and tilt his head and drink. . . . He felt in his hunger a deep sense of duty, as powerful as the urge to breathe, as intimate as the beat of his heart. . . . He wanted to pull off his clothes and roll in the snow until something nourishing seeped into his body through the pores of his skin. He wanted to grip something in his hands so hard that it would turn to food.

But the terrible honesty of *Native Son* was its acknowledgment that people to whom life has been denied can only learn contempt from those who deny them. (Wright understood how effective could be the fascists' appeal to unappeased resentment.) And so Bigger begins to live through a kind of aesthetics of hate:

> He was living, truly and deeply, no matter what others might think, looking at him with their blind eyes. Never had he had

the chance to live out the consequences of his actions; never had his will been so free as in this night and day of fear and murder and flight.

For Bigger there is an almost erotic pleasure in seeing his picture in the papers, and his terror mixes with thrill while he watches from the rooftop as the white mobs converge upon him. He has provoked them, enraged them, even eluded and confounded them. After a lifetime of being owned, he now possesses them.

Bigger's sensory awakening is a version of Wright's own (right down to the consoling taste of warm milk), which he describes in *Black Boy*:

The days and hours began to speak now with a clearer tongue. Each experience had a meaning of its own. . . . There was the drenching hospitality in the pervading smell of sweet magnolias. . . . There was the dry hot summer morning when I scratched my bare arms on briers while picking blackberries and came home with my fingers and lips stained black with sweet berry juice. . . . There was the drugged, sleepy feeling that came from sipping glasses of milk, drinking them slowly so that they would last a long time, and drinking enough for the first time in my life.

For Wright, the resurrection of his senses was a liberating event, benign and even gentle, evoked in almost pantheistic terms borrowed from Walt Whitman. For Bigger, it is the discovery that he has the power to damage and destroy white lives.

In 1940 Bigger's was an almost unwritable violence. Explosive, indiscriminate, he finds he has a taste for killing; hours after burn-

ing Mary Dalton's body in the furnace he crushes Bessie's head
with a brick, this black woman whom he both loves for her tenderness and hates for her despair. Wright's editors and sponsors
worried that this squalid story might prove unreadable. They were
wrong. *Native Son* sold 215,000 copies in three weeks—in a world
poised on the verge of a conflagration in which the human capacity for systematic and spontaneous violence would be proven
larger than anyone dreamed.

Wright had invented a young black man who awakens to himself by discovering his capacity for rage, by punching through the
racial wall into moments of bodily contact (carnal and lethal) that
confirm the aliveness of his body. In the autobiography that he
wrote five years later, Wright makes it clear that he too had found
salvation in the life of the body. He recalls the electric moments
when, in his early days as a dishwasher in Chicago, a white wait-
ress brushed casually against him without complaint, and when
another turned to him for intimate help:

> One summer morning a white girl came late to work and
> rushed into the pantry where I was busy. She went into the
> women's room and changed her clothes; I heard the door
> open and seconds later I was surprised to hear her voice:
> "Richard, quick! Tie my apron!"
> She was standing with her back to me and the strings of
> her apron dangled loose. There was a moment of indecision
> on my part, then I took the two loose strings and carried
> them around her body and brought them again to her back
> and tied them in a clumsy knot.
> "Thanks a million," she said grasping my hand for a split
> second, and was gone.

In the South this incandescent moment would have been read by virtually any observer as a hint of potential miscegenation. But Wright discovered a new world in Chicago, a place not where taboos could be broken but where the dividing line of race could simply be forgotten in the press of daily life. He delighted in Chicago because it occasionally offered anonymity: "It was strange to pause before a crowded newsstand and buy a newspaper without having to wait until a white man was served." And it was wonderfully strange to ride the trolley beside a white man who, instead of pulling away, "was still staring out the window, his mind fastened on some inward thought. I did not exist for him; I was as far from his mind as the stone buildings that swept past in the street."

In the mid-1940s Wright moved to Paris ("city of refuge," he called it) and became part of the literary circle that included Gertrude Stein (whose "Melanctha" had been an early influence) and André Gide, as well as leading intellectuals of the "Negritude" movement—Léopold Senghor, Aimé Césaire, and others. Wright, in turn, gave encouragement and patronage to younger black American writers such as James Baldwin and Chester Himes. By the early 1950s he was devoting himself to a new novel, *The Outsider* (1953)—the story of a black intellectual who begins life with a new identity after being presumed dead in a train wreck. Wright composed this novel, whose theme is the exhilarating loss of a burdensome self, under the personal influence of Jean-Paul Sartre and Simone de Beauvoir and after considerable reading in Heidegger and Husserl; it contained a bitter attack on the Communist Party as a purveyor of false messianic hope.

This was also true of the second section of Wright's autobiography, which he agreed to drop, again at the behest of the Book-of-the-Month Club, and which was only published after his death under the original title of the whole work, *American Hunger* (it is now reattached to *Black Boy* in the Library of America edition). Like *The Outsider*, it is a candid record of Wright's disillusionment with the Communist promise. He blamed the Party for intervening with friends at the book club to drop the offending section of his memoir, but he acceded to the pressure, though he published some of the deleted chapters separately—including one long section, "I Tried to Be a Communist," that appeared in *The Atlantic* and was widely read in Richard Crossman's notable anthology of works by ex-Communists about their experience with the Party, *The God That Failed* (1950).

In 1954 his publishers brought out *Savage Holiday*, Wright's novel about a white psychopathic murderer, which was well received in France but pretty much ignored at home. By now he was becoming a little formulaic in his demonstration of savagery—this time not beneath the servility of a black youth but just below the civility of a middle-class white man. Then Wright reverted to his native Mississippi for the setting of his last novel, *The Long Dream* (1958). Spanning the decade from the end of World War II to the height of McCarthyism, all of this writing has sporadic power and historical interest. But his artistic imagination had, I think, been nearly exhausted by *Native Son*—the book in which he had faced up to the blood-dread between whites and blacks and, in horror and sorrow, had shown how impervious it was to rationalist solutions offered by both reformers and radicals.

Wright did not want to believe in the intractability of the prob-

lem. He felt himself fleetingly released from it among the wait-
resses in the Chicago kitchen, and even in *Native Son* he reached
for themes that transcend it. His early stories, as Baldwin remarked after his death, "did not make me think . . . particularly
of Negroes. They made me think of human loss and helplessness."
One of the rewards of coming back after years to *Native Son* is
to see how reductive it is to read it as merely a tract about race.
It can be read as a transcription of an adolescent dream, as a
portrait of a man for whom guilt is a half-formed emotion, as a
critique of philanthropic sentimentality.

Native Son is also a prescient anticipation of contemporary insights into the pathologies of the ghetto family and of the indictment of black men, lately handed down in black feminist writing,
for punishing black women in recompense for their stolen dignity.
It is certainly, too, a tour de force of psychological manipulation:
when the bloodhound reporters, milling about in the Daltons'
overheated basement, tell Bigger to clear out the ashes to quiet
the furnace, we shudder with him as Mary's unconsumed bones
drop down through the grate. Our allegiance is with Bigger, even
as we apprehend more and more of his animal ferocity.

"Shattering" is a critical word that has been properly consigned
to service as an adjective in blurbs. But there *is* a whole class of
books for which this word, or some synonym that conveys the
idea that a book can do real violence to the mind, is indispensable.
Not all great books work by this kind of assault, but some do, and
thereby they are fatal to whatever mental structure the reader
inhabits when he sits down to read them. *Native Son* is such a
book. It is all the more remarkable because it achieves its destructive power not by exposing the inadequacies of conventional
thinking but by dramatizing conventional ideas in such a way that

they can never be held casually again. *Native Son* was indeed the book Wright swore to write so that "no one would weep over it," the book that "would be so hard and deep" that it would deny its readers "the consolation of tears." It was the first book that forced Americans to take their racial fears seriously, and it did so by turning their most vicious thoughts against themselves.

It is a profound irony that the arc of Wright's career moved downward after *Native Son* because of his refusal to be imprisoned by the thematics of race. His move to France, where he partook of the prestige attached to the man of color in exile from the crass United States, did not enlarge him as a writer. He became, perhaps, a more cosmopolitan artist. Still, as Baldwin said, speaking from within the same paradox, Paris "would not have been a city of refuge for us if we had not been armed with American passports," and "it did not seem worthwhile to me to have fled the native fantasy only to embrace a foreign one."

In his moving eulogy, Baldwin reflected that Wright was "one of the most illustrious victims" of "the war in the breast between blackness and whiteness." Writing in the heady atmosphere of postcolonial possibility, Baldwin added that "it is no longer important to be white—thank heaven—the white face is no longer invested with the power of this world; and it is devoutly to be hoped that it will soon no longer be important to be black." Such a dissolution of difference was Wright's hope, too. All his work was a plea that racial identity be submerged in the colorless fact of being human. But his enduring greatness as an artist will be owed, I think, to his unprecedented ability to convey the horror of being black in America. What he wished for was to lose his subject. After reading *Native Son*, no one can doubt his willingness to make the sacrifice.

11

The Political Incorrectness
of Zora Neale Hurston

In the 1930s, Zora Neale Hurston was among the Negro darlings of New York white society. Of all the "Niggerati," as Langston Hughes put it, she was "certainly the most amusing." Having come to town in 1925 at the suggestion of her instructors at Howard University (where she had taken classes while working as a maid and manicurist), she burst into the circle of black writers and the white patrons whom they escorted to Harlem nightspots. She signed her letters to white friends "Your pickaninny, Zora," and was known for her flamboyance, her pranks (she once lifted subway fare from a beggar's cup, with a promise to repay him later), and her brazen talk. "I never expect to have a greater thrill than that wire gave me" was how she remembered receiving the telegram informing her that J. B. Lippincott would publish her first novel, *Jonah's Gourd Vine* (1934). "You know the feeling when you found your first pubic hair. Greater than that."

It was at Barnard College, which Hurston attended on a scholarship arranged by one of her benefactors, that she learned that the rural black speech with which she had grown up in the South was an object of anthropological interest for white intellectuals. At Barnard she became a protégée of the revered anthropologist Franz Boas, whom, to the delight of his cowed white students, she called "Papa Franz" to his face. Charmed by her insolence and intelligence, Boas dispatched her to Harlem, where she was assigned the task of disproving theories of Negro inferiority by measuring the skulls of pedestrians. Then he sent her South to collect lore.

After graduation, Hurston became, like many talented writers in the early 1930s, a kind of vagabond reporter, subsisting on fellowships arranged by Boas and on a stipend provided by one of her New York patrons. The understanding was, as she put it in her autobiography, *Dust Tracks on a Road* (1942), that she would "tell the tales, sing the songs, do the dances, and repeat the raucous sayings and doings of the Negro farthest down." In Florida, Louisiana, and the West Indies, she gathered material that she would eventually use in *Jonah's Gourd Vine*, a fictional reconstruction of her parents' lives in the black community of Eatonville, Florida, and in her folklore collections, *Mules and Men* (1935) and *Tell My Horse* (1938).

Her life, she reported later, "was in danger several times . . . [because] primitive minds are quick to sunshine and quick to anger." While on the road she sometimes lived in her car (which she named "Sassie Susie"), carried a revolver (pearl-handled) when the situation seemed to require it, and sent off an occasional sketch for publication. "In one case," as she later recalled, about a Hoodoo initiation ceremony in New Orleans, ". . . I lay naked for three days and nights on a couch, with my navel to a rattle-snake skin which had been dressed and dedicated to the ceremony." By the mid-1930s, Hurston had a recognized byline in academic journals, where she published articles on Negro dance and musical traditions, and in general magazines, to which she contributed profiles and reviews. With the publication in 1937 of *Their Eyes Were Watching God*, a novel of great vitality and erotic power that she wrote "under internal pressure in seven weeks" while researching religious practices in Haiti, she became a minor literary celebrity.

In much of her writing, Hurston was preoccupied with the destructive force of love, which renders a woman vulnerable to a man who cannot subdue his compulsive need for new conquests. Testing this theme in *Jonah's Gourd Vine*, in which she told the tale of her father's inconstancy, she explored the proximity of passion to violence for a black man whose sphere of authority is circumscribed within a domestic circle, outside of which he controls nothing. She understood how a wife becomes both an idol and a torment to such a man. "Ain't never no man tuh breathe in yo' face but me," says John to his wife in *Jonah's Gourd Vine*, with a threat that comes from the depth of his soul. If she deceives him, "Ahm goin' tuh kill you jes' ez sho ez gun is iron."

In *Their Eyes Were Watching God*, Hurston relinquished the mobility of the omniscient narrator who had moved in *Jonah's Gourd Vine* between the consciousnesses of husband and wife. In the new novel she continued to write in the third person, but the voice speaks almost exclusively from within the mind of the woman who stands at the center of the tale, Janie Crawford. This is a book of extremely intimate emotion, "dammed up in me," as Hurston later put it, until she found the form into which it could be released. She had broken off an affair with a much younger West Indian man (she was nearly forty when they met, he was twenty-three) with whom she had been "soaked . . . in ecstasy," but who had had fixed ideas about a woman's dependency to which she could not bring herself to conform. *Their Eyes Were Watching God* is, in part, a testament to their doomed passion.

Like *Jonah's Gourd Vine*, the new book is set in a world in which white people exist only as flickering shadows. But there is a more vivid sense of their oppressive presence, too, a sense of how hard it is for any black family to make a dignified life out of scraps from the white man's table. Janie, raised by a grandmother who was born into slavery and raped by her master, is the repository of the old woman's dreams and the object of her protection. At the first sign of Janie's sexual awakening—which Hurston evokes beautifully in a scene where the girl "stretched on her back beneath the pear tree soaking in the alto chant of the visiting bees . . . [and watched] a dust-bearing bee sink into the sanctum of a bloom"—her grandmother arranges a marriage to a respectable farmer. He is a solid man who chops enough wood to keep the stove hot and "keeps both water buckets full." When the girl objects that she feels nothing for him—"But Nanny, Ah wants to want him sometimes. Ah don't want him to do all de wantin' "—she is admonished for her romantic fantasies, for feeling that he is "desecrating the pear tree" in which she had beheld "the thousand sister-calyxes arch to meet the love embrace" of the bee.

Later, after she has endured two dutiful marriages, Janie explains her grandmother's thinking to a friend:

> [Nanny] was borned in slavery time when folks, dat is black folks, didn't sit down anytime dey felt lak it. So sittin' on porches lak de white madam looked lak uh mighty fine thing tuh her. Dat's whut she wanted for me—don't keer whut it

cost. Git up on uh high chair and sit dere. She didn't have time tuh think whut tuh do after you got up on de stool uh do nothin'. De object wuz tuh git dere. So Ah got up on de high stool lak she told me, but Pheoby, Ah done nearly languished tuh death up dere. Ah felt like de world wuz cryin' extry and Ah ain't read de common news yet.

This is Janie's retrospective account of how she had become parched in the keeping of her first husband and why, when Joe Starks, "a cityfied, stylish dressed man," coaxed her away from her servitude, she jumped at the chance.

But life with Starks turns out to be just another episode of stool-sitting, this time behind the counter of his general store, where he installs her as a decorative clerk. "The spirit of the marriage left the bedroom and took to living in the parlor. It was there to shake hands whenever company came to visit, but it never went back inside the bedroom again." Hurston often described with cruel precision the slackening of a man's body ("he had let his waistline go a bit," she wrote about her West Indian lover, "and that bespoke his inside feeling"), but she always preserved enough sympathy to catch the hints of fear and self-hatred in his expression as he watches the damage inflicted by time:

One day she noticed that Joe didn't sit down. He just stood in front of a chair and fell in it. . . . He didn't rear back in his knees any longer. He squatted over his ankles when he walked. . . . His prosperous-looking belly that used to thrust out so pugnaciously and intimidate folks, sagged like a load suspended from his loins. It didn't seem to be part of him anymore. Eyes a little absent too.

When Starks dies, Janie, now a woman in her forties, pines again for the kind of "self-crushing love" she has felt only as an unquenched longing.

"Self-crushing love" finally arrives in the form of a young man known as Tea-Cake. A drifter in his twenties, he seems "a glance from God," as if he were "crushing scent out of the world with his footsteps." Even as she is drawn to him, Janie is warned and scolded and clucked at by her friends. Her grandmother's lesson—that love is "de very prong all of us black women gits hung on"—is rehearsed for her again. She has learned from her own experience, after all, that a man's ministrations to her desire can be just a spasm between stretches of indifference or abuse. So at first she withholds herself, suspecting that Tea-Cake's professions of hot love are merely "night thought[s]" and that he will resume his cool scheming in the morning.

As love overwhelms Janie and sweeps her along toward tragedy, Hurston fills the novel with glimpses of women who have been destroyed by falling for younger men—Annie Tyler, for instance, "who at 52 had been left a widow with a good home and insurance money." Wearing "under-sized high-heel slippers [that] were punishing her tired feet," she runs off with a young flatterer, "her body squeezed and crowded into a tight corset that shoved her middle up under her chin." Then, a few weeks later, she turns up discarded, with "all the capers that cheap dye could cut . . . showing in her hair . . . her hanging bosom and stomach and buttocks and legs . . . draped down over her ankles." In this image Janie sees a premonition of herself.

After the exertion of writing *Their Eyes Were Watching God*, Hurston had two more novels in her. The first, published in 1939, was *Moses, Man of the Mountain*, a zany burlesque of the Book of Exodus that recasts the prophet as a kind of jive godfather. Ever since she had been captivated as a child by the stories of the Old Testament, Hurston had admired the Jews for having "a God who laid about Him when they needed Him":

I came to start reading the Bible through my mother. She gave me a licking one afternoon for repeating something I had overheard a neighbor telling her. She locked me in her room after the whipping, and the Bible was the only thing in there for me to read. I happened to open to the place where David was doing some mighty smiting, and I got interested. David went here and he went there, and no matter where he went, he smote 'em hip and thigh. Then he sung songs to his harp a while, and went out and smote some more. Not one time did David stop and preach about sins and things. All David wanted to know from God was who to kill and when. He took care of the other details himself. I liked him a lot.

Now, with a kind of antic reverence, she expropriated the story of the Jews' redemption under Moses as an exemplum for contemporary black life. The trouble is, she retells it with a mix of bombast and parody that one would expect from a collaborative screenplay by Cecil B. DeMille and Spike Lee. It becomes a blackface farce: "We remember the nice fresh fish we used to get back there in Egypt every day," the grumbling Jews recall about the good old days under Pharaoh. "Nice sweet-tasting little pan-fish and a person could get all they could eat for five cents. Unhunh! . . . and the leeks and onions and plenty garlic for seasoning!"

And nearly ten years later, in 1948, came *Seraph on the Su-*

wanee, a psychological portrait of a white couple, of which Hurston's biographer, Robert Hemenway, has aptly said that its main male character "becomes a shrimp-boat captain for the sole purpose of demonstrating Hurston's knowledge of shrimping."

As Hurston lost her bearings as an artist, her personal life fell apart too. Her relations became strained with her chief patron, Charlotte Mason, who held publication rights to the materials that Hurston had gathered on her expeditions in the South and who balked at her plan to adapt them for commercial theatrical performance. In the mid-1940s, Lippincott rejected two novels, one about wealthy blacks, the other set in Eatonville; and various other projects, including a biography of Herod the Great (for which she invited Winston Churchill to write an introduction), never came to fruition. After two short-lived marriages and an aborted engagement, she was falsely accused of molesting a young boy. Although the case was dismissed after an investigation, she never quite recovered, and spent her last years in ill health, working as a maid, an office clerk, and a substitute teacher. She died impoverished, in a Florida welfare home, in 1960.

If this life is a sad tale of talent dissipated, the posthumous career of Hurston's reputation is an entirely different story. Since the late 1970s, when she was acknowledged as an exemplary genius by a rising group of black women writers (Alice Walker arranged for a headstone to be placed in the cemetery where Hurston had been buried in an unmarked grave), her work has become a fixture in anthologies and on college reading lists. And now that the Library of America has issued a two-volume edition of her collected work, her status as a classic seems secure.

The fluctuations of Hurston's reputation constitute a precise register of the mood not only of American literary culture in the twentieth century but of the racial attitudes that have accounted for an important part of its context. In the 1920s and 1930s she was a curiosity, a brainy black girl who could coax "her people" to talk the old lingo so that it might be written down and preserved before it disappeared. Franz Boas, whose other students included Ruth Benedict and Margaret Mead and who had, according to Hurston, "no pet wishes to prove," was a forward-looking man skeptical of received platitudes about racial difference. But he was also trafficking in old notions about the distinction between deracinated city dwellers and country people whose ideas, as Jane Addams (writing about the "South Italian peasant") had put it at the turn of the century, "have come directly . . . from their struggle with nature."

What Boas had at hand a few blocks from Columbia was a living laboratory stocked by the post–World War I migration of rural Southern blacks to the Northern metropolis. And what Addams had said of her transplanted Italians seemed to apply equally well (if one substitutes cotton and tobacco for "olives and oranges") to the Negro. Country virtues become city vices:

[He] comes from a life of picking olives and oranges, and he easily sends his children out to pick up coal from railroad tracks, or wood from buildings which have been burned down. Unfortunately . . . it is easy to go from the coal on the railroad track to the coal and wood which stands before a dealer's shop; from the potatoes which have rolled from a rumbling wagon to the vegetables displayed by the grocer.

For Boas and his colleagues, Zora Hurston was not only a useful agent for satisfying his own curiosity about this dislocated people but also a willing object of it. "From the earliest rocking of my cradle," she wrote in *Mules and Men*,

> I had known about the capers Brer Rabbit is apt to cut and what the Squinch Owl says from the house top. But it was fitting me like a tight chemise. I couldn't see it for wearing it. It was only when I was off in college, away from my native surroundings, that I could see myself like somebody else and stand off and look at my garment. Then I had to have the spy-glass of Anthropology to look through at that.

With Hurston having agreed to serve Boas as a kind of espionage agent spying on herself, it is not surprising that her first debunkers were black. Alain Locke, her own teacher from her days at Howard, urged her to stop trying to distract white readers with amusing folktales and to turn instead to "social document" fiction. To some readers, Hurston's folklore collections seemed sanitized. *"Mules and Men,"* wrote Sterling Brown, "should be more bitter; it would be nearer the total truth" if, for every comic story about a long-winded preacher or bumbling cuckold, there was an account of a beating or a lynching—experiences that were, after all, also preserved in black oral culture. Richard Wright was even blunter, decrying Hurston's "minstrel technique that makes the white folks laugh."

By the mid-1940s, Roy Wilkins was publicly attacking Hurston as a peddler of nostalgia for the Jim Crow South, where happy darkies putatively sang and danced on the farm. Ever since, this implication that she pandered to white fantasies has remained a steady theme in Hurston criticism. In the 1970s, the historian Nathan Huggins called her a professional "folk" Negro, and, more recently, Ann Douglas, in *Terrible Honesty: Mongrel Manhattan in the 1920s* (1995), judged her an exception to the approbation implicit in her title. Hurston, she writes, "played shamelessly" to rich whites who fancied themselves the champions and guardians of "black vitality."

These critics have a point. Some of Hurston's characters run uncomfortably close to white-manufactured racial stereotypes. The young Joe Starks in *Their Eyes Were Watching God* is a dandy with "silk sleeveholders" who could step without a costume change into *Porgy and Bess* (1935) as a stand-in for Sportin' Life. And the sycophantic women who come into Starks's store, "running a little, caressing a little and all the time making little urging-on cries" as he and his wife dispense delicacies from behind the counter, would make any casting director think of Butterfly McQueen.

And yet Hurston was not finally a trader in stock types. She did furnish her novels with long passages of tall-tale telling, and there are too many moments of Amos 'n' Andy buffoonery; but she refused to visit what she called the "museum . . . dedicated to the convenient 'typical,' "

[where] there is the "typical" Oriental, Jew, Yankee, Westerner, Southerner, Latin, and even out-of-favor Nordics like the German. The Englishman "I say, old chappie," and the gesticulating Frenchman [live there, and] the American Negro exhibit is a group of two. Both of these mechanical toys

are built so that their feet eternally shuffle, and their eyes pop and roll. Shuffling feet and those popping, rolling eyes denote the Negro, and no characterization is genuine without this monotony. One is seated on a stump picking away on his banjo and singing and laughing. The other is a most amoral character before a share-cropper's shack mumbling about injustice.

The real reason that Hurston's reputation declined between the 1940s and the 1970s was that as the civil rights movement led most intellectuals to regard Southern black folk culture as a residual symptom of slavery and segregation, the curatorial impulse of the 1930s, when Hurston had traveled with Alan Lomax, collecting samples of black folk music for the Library of Congress, gave way to the imperatives of integration and assimilation. Hurston's characters, who tend to speak in dialect, became faintly embarrassing. Her affection for the sealed black world in which she had grown up came to seem, in other words, politically retrograde.

But Hurston's politics had never been coherent, and it is a mistake, really, to take her opinions too seriously. She tended to shoot off letters to the editor or to blurt things out in interviews. Thus in 1943, tired of liberal patronizing, she remarked that "the lot of the Negro is much better in the South than in the North" and even went so far as to say to a reporter that "the Jim Crow system works," a statement that Wilkins characterized in *The Amsterdam News* as "arrant, even vicious nonsense." But only a year earlier she had written (in a passage in *Dust Tracks on a Road* that was deleted by her Lippincott editors but is now restored in the Library of America edition):

President Roosevelt could extend his four freedoms to some
people right here in America. . . . I am not bitter, but I see
what I see. He can call names across an ocean, but he evi-
dently has not the courage to speak even softly at home. . . .
I will fight for my country but I will not lie for her.

And two years later she attacked the "the Jim Crow laws" for
confining black people to "back seats in trains, [and] back doors
of houses" where "the smallest dark child is to be convinced of
its inferiority."

By the 1950s, Hurston had settled into a belligerent conserva-
tism. She supported the presidential candidacy of Robert Taft.
Construing the motives of black integrationists as a form of race
embarrassment, she opposed the Supreme Court decision in
Brown v. *Board of Education.* "I saw no curse in being black,"
she had written in *Dust Tracks on a Road,* "nor no extra flavor
by being white. I saw no benefit in excusing my looks by claiming
to be half Indian." These are sensible sentences when read as
comments on a certain kind of shame that takes root among people who have been trained in self-contempt. But when she offered
the same sort of sentiment as a defense of segregated schools—
"I can see no tragedy in being too dark to be invited to a white
school social affair"—she revealed only her political naiveté, and
consigned herself to oblivion for another decade.

In the late 1960s and 1970s, when a new aesthetic of racial
pride emerged (always with a tinge of separatism), her reputation
began to recover. "By the '60s," as Alice Walker wrote in 1976,
"everyone understood that black women could wear beautiful
cloths on their beautiful heads and care about the authenticity of
things cullud *and* African." Zora had been there first. And so

Walker commended her to a new generation of readers, especially black women, for her sense of "racial health—a sense of black people as complete, complex [and] *undiminished*" on their own terms.

It was in those years that Hurston the ethnographer and Hurston the segregationist gave way to Hurston the feminist. To students today, one of the most familiar passages in all of American literature is the grandmother's speech to Janie about the hard hierarchy of the world:

> Honey, de white man is de ruler of everything as fur as Ah been able tuh find out. Maybe it's some place way off in de ocean where de black man is in power, but we don't know nothin' but what we see. So de white man throw down de load and tell de nigger man tuh pick it up. He pick it up because he have to, but he don't tote it. He hand it to his womenfolks. De nigger woman is de mule uh de world so fur as Ah can see.

When one reads the stories that substantiate this passage, it becomes obvious that the feminist reclamation of Zora Neale Hurston was well-founded and overdue. Critics such as Wright had missed the essence of her vision, which was "documentary" and realistic from the point of view of black women, who tended to be subsidiary characters or glanced-at props in Wright's own fiction. Hurston was most compelling when she wrote about the plight of a black woman as the object of sexual exploitation by a white man, or as the focal point on which a black man concentrates his diffuse anger. "Ah can't die easy," Janie's grandmother says to the unpolluted child, "thinkin' maybe de menfolks white or black is makin' a spit cup outa you." What seemed to some readers her preoccupation with sex was really a candid acknowledgment that, especially for black women, the craving for bodily pleasure was both an intimation of transcendence and a form of imprisonment.

Still, as long as Hurston remains susceptible to what are essentially political judgments (the feminist approval was oddly symmetrical with the disapproval thirty years earlier by Locke and Wright), her literary fortunes will continue to fluctuate with the temper of the times. Writing in the academic idiom of the 1990s, the critic Hazel Carby has recently charged that Hurston is a writer who "privileges the nostalgic and freezes it in time." At a time when millions of black Americans are coping with despair in the inner city, Carby asks, "[Has] *Their Eyes Were Watching God* become the most frequently taught black novel because it acts as a mode of assurance that, really, the black folk are happy and healthy?"

This is an apposite question. The trouble, as with all criticism that restricts itself to questions about reception or ideology, is that it misses the basic reason the writer is worth reading in the first place. Hurston belongs among the American classics not because of her politics but because of her language. She was at pains to distinguish herself from "the great horde of individuals known as 'Race champions,'" to whom "no Negro exists as an individual— he exists only as another tragic unit of the Race." Some writers, Hurston charged, think there is bravery

in following the groove of the Race champions, when the truth is, it is the line of least resistance and least originality— certain to be approved of by the 'champions' who want to hear the same thing over and over again even though they already know it by heart, and certain to be unread by everybody else. It is the same thing as waving the flag in a poorly constructed play.

Hurston's saving distinction was her exquisitely sensitive ear. She was sometimes out of tune, as when she tried to devise metaphors that were self-consciously literary ("there is a basin in the mind where words float around"). But when she deployed colloquial black speech and celebrated its ability to move beyond mere denotation, she was a spectacular writer, and the farthest thing from a flag waver. When, for instance, she describes a speeding train in *Jonah's Gourd Vine*, she uses a word that perfectly conveys the sound of the wheels clicking over the track joints: it "schickalacked" over the rails. A girl walks "hippily" past a porch full of gaping men. A woman is only "mouf glad" rather than "sho nuff glad" when she tries to deflect with a forced smile her man's gathering anger. The phrase "sense you intuh it" functions as a verb that works much better than "tell" or "explain" to express how words transmit images and feeling from speaker to hearer.

Hurston was a brilliant transcriber of dialect, but this was only part of her achievement. When writing in her own voice, she renders the world in phrases that are palpable and wonderfully immediate; her mind moves rapidly from the general proposition ("there was nothing then to hinder impulses") to the particular illustration ("they didn't have zippers on pants in those days, guaranteed to stay locked no matter what the strain"). Here, by assembling a sequence of complementary images, she expresses the cost to her father of her mother's judgment that he had been born coarse and vulgar and had needed to be refined:

I know now that it is a griping thing to a man—not to be able to whip his woman mentally. Some women know how to give their man that conquesting feeling. My mother took her over-the-creek man and bare-knuckled him from brogans to broadcloth, and I am certain that he was proud of the change, in public. But in the house, he might have always felt over-the-creek, and because this was not the statue he had made for himself to look at, he resented it.

This is a writer who understood that spontaneous image-making is the mark of a living language, that a shared language is the only conduit we have into the interior life of other people. In an essay in 1950 called "What White Publishers Won't Print," Hurston explains what drove her as an artist: the conviction that the writer must reveal the most intimate experiences of persons who have been looked upon as types. Through such revelations, the reader who has not been completely lost to the dishonesty of prejudice will recognize a common human bond:

Argue all you will or may about injustice, but as long as the majority cannot conceive of a Negro or a Jew feeling and reacting inside just as they do, the majority will keep right on believing that people who do not look like them cannot possibly feel as they do, and conform to the established pattern. It is well known that there must be a body of waived matter, let us say, things accepted and taken for granted by all in a community before there can be that commonality of feeling. The usual phrase is having things in common. Until this is thoroughly established in respect to Negroes in America, as well as other minorities, it will remain impossible for the majority to conceive of a Negro experiencing a deep and abiding love and not just the passion of sex. That a great mass of Negroes can be stirred by the pageants of Spring and Fall; the extravaganza of summer, and the majesty of winter. That they can and do experience discovery of the numerous subtle faces as a foundation for a great and selfless love . . .

Hurston's real subject, and this is the reason her work will abide, was the universal disjunction between the limitless human imagination and the constrictions within which all human beings live their lives. She happened to know best how to exemplify this theme by writing about the lives of black women in the American South which in itself is cause for neither praise nor blame. She was caught in the paradox in which all major black American writers have been caught: she wished to honor her people by recording their uniquely tragic experience while at the same time refusing to cordon off that experience from the universal human condition of hope and dread.

Hurston rejected all the conventional categories—race, class, gender—by which some of her latest critics organize experience. Finally, she was not a Negro writer or (as she might be classified today) a "subaltern" writer or a woman writer. "Negroes are supposed to write about the Race Problem," she says in *Dust Tracks on a Road*. "I was and am thoroughly sick of the subject. My interest lies in what makes a man or a woman do such-and-so, regardless of his color."

12

Reading for Pleasure

When I was a college student twenty-five years ago, I enrolled in a popular course in the history of literary criticism. On the final exam, along with admonitions not to treat the same author repeatedly or to cluster our answers in one or two centuries (the course had run from Aristotle to R. P. Blackmur), the professor printed in uppercase letters the following piece of advice: TES-TIMONIALS OF DELIGHT WILL NOT SUFFICE.

In most universities today, this warning is no longer necessary. A final exam is now more likely to resemble a pathology test in medical school—an assessment of one's ability to identify through a textual sample what ails the culture that produced it. The inventory of possible disorders includes misogyny, racism, homophobia, imperialist arrogance, as well as more insidious conditions like gender anxiety or an unconscious longing to absorb the "Other." Reporting recently in a journal published by the Modern Language Association (the guild to which most literature professors belong), the critic Morris Dickstein gives an unfortunately plausible account of an instructor who begins each class with the question: "All right, what's wrong with this book?" When I hear this sort of thing echoed even by undergraduates—who are generally eager for new pleasures and resentful of those who would foreclose them—I become very discouraged about my profession. We have turned literary texts into excretions through which, while holding our noses, we search for traces of the maladies of our culture. It is no wonder that testimonials of delight are no longer a problem.

How did we come to this situation? Observers on the right might say (or at least think) that it is the result of social changes that have swept through institutions of higher learning. Everyone who teaches in a tradition-minded institution knows what this means. We all have had the experience of sitting around the table with colleagues in whose ranks women and racial minorities are better represented than they once were, while the white male worthies of the past (in my university they have names like Fairchild and Krapp) glare down from their portraits like dowagers at an orgy. This sea change in the social composition of our profession is as dramatic as it is overdue. But it does not account for what has happened to the relation between the profession and its putative subject, literature—namely, the fact that we used to like it and now do not seem to like it anymore.

The social explanation for this change is not helpful. It belies the fact that if literary appreciation flourishes anywhere these days, it is in the new fields of feminism, gay studies, and ethnic studies, where leading critics still engage in the old-fashioned work of discovering, promoting, and relishing new texts, or forging new relations with old ones. The joy that some of these critics take in their reading is an emotion that can be sustained only in a mood of assent to one's material. Theirs is the pleasure of discovering that words are a kind of depository where forbidden feelings can be kept safe until a kindred reader comes along to receive and revive them. The recent outpouring of gay criticism on writers such as Melville and Thoreau, for example, amounts to a celebration that someone whose fraternity was long concealed has at last been recognized. He who has been lost is found; and these critics announce the prodigal's return in an exclamatory, ingenuous voice that is entirely different from what one usually hears in the academy.

Yet with all the delight that one still finds in certain corners of the university, there is a fundamental *literary* pleasure from which almost all varieties of criticism have become estranged. This is the pleasure derived from what Emerson calls "the accidency and fugacity of the symbol"—the pleasure one feels, for instance, when Melville likens the wreckage of a whale boat to bits of nutmeg swirling in a stirred bowl of punch. It is the pleasure of surprising conjunctions, as in Miltonic phrases like "darkness visible" and "palpable obscure," that startle us and make us hear commonplace words as if they had just been invented. "The use of symbols," says Emerson, "has a certain power of emancipation and exhilaration for all men." Yet this feeling of release is precisely what much criticism today seems set against. Do we still recognize ourselves in Emerson's dictum that the "metamorphosis" of the world by the imagination "excites in the beholder an emotion of joy"? Can we still say that "we seem to be touched by a wand which makes us dance and run about happily, like children"?

Too seldom, I think. For a number of years in a graduate seminar I teach on Melville, the session devoted to style worked least well. The students hummed along through our thematic discussions, talking fluently and intelligently about Melville's views of colonialism, sexuality, and class relations, as well as about more abstract issues such as his understanding of the relation between perception and expression. But when we turned to style, they tended to grow quiet and look down at the table. From my colleagues who teach mainly poetry, I understand that even the most sophisticated students still tend to have little idea about prosody and are not quite sure why it should matter.

This is not a case of fallen standards. Graduate students are more precociously professional than ever before. But by and large, under the sway of teachers from my own generation, they do not become aspiring professors in the old religious sense of that word: believers, testifiers, witnesses. Lately, I have noticed some signs that this may be beginning to change—hints of a revival of interest in what lifts a style out of the pedestrian and makes it distinguished. If I am right, our students are ahead of us, because my own generation seems permanently marked by the spirit of the 1970s, when literature, which had been celebrated by the "New Critics" in the 1950s as a counter-universe to the spiritually barren world in which they found themselves living, and by the "Myth Critics" in the 1960s as a way of entering the unconscious life, first came to be widely thought of as not a sphere of beauty but an instrument of power.

In the waning years of the Vietnam War and its bitter aftermath, literature was revealed as just another means by which we are indoctrinated into pernicious doctrines like patriarchy and progress. We were invited to study books as a part of the state apparatus. Literature began to be talked about with metaphors of incarceration—as a "prison-house of language" or a "hermeneutic circle." Culture came to be thought of as totalitarian, and books, no less than gulags, became instruments of domination. What was lost, along with our capacity for pleasure, was our sense of proportion, our humor, and our common sense.

As these changes took hold, some people had the tact to recognize that what was going on should no longer be called literary criticism. It required a new name. So we renamed ourselves practitioners of *cultural studies*. What the cultural critic does is to identify the structures within which we once lived unreflectively. Although many such critics have good literary instincts, there is nothing intrinsically literary about their subject: the cultural studies method can be as well applied to newscasts or cartoons as to novels and plays. One of its purposes is to detach old terms from ideas to which they have belonged for so long that they have come to seem God-given rather than man-made. So, for instance, words like "male" and "female," which once seemed innocuous terms for natural conditions, are revealed as the names by which our culture assigns appropriate behaviors to the two biologically distinct entities that comprise the human race.

The disposition of mind that I have been describing did not spring up out of nowhere, of course. It had many philosophical antecedents; Martin Heidegger and Jacques Derrida were only the most frequently cited. In America, its roots run deep into the pragmatist tradition associated with Charles Sanders Peirce, William James, John Dewey, and, most recently, Richard Rorty—a tradition in which truth has always been understood as changeable in accordance with our descriptions of the world. "Reality," in the pragmatic view, is not a fixed entity—an essence, as we say nowadays—capable of being revealed. It is, rather, an unstable zone between phenomena that are unknowable in themselves and the innumerable fields of mental activity (which we call persons) by which they are apprehended. The name we give to these apprehensions is consciousness. And consciousness is not an entity, but a ceaseless process in which the reception of new impressions is indistinguishable from the production of new meanings.

These basic assumptions underlie the view of culture that became commonplace in the 1970s and that now dominates many classrooms. Here is one example from the theorist Fredric Jameson: "Consciousness [is] a kind of construction rather than a stable substance . . . a locus of relationships rather than an ego in the older sense." This postmodernist view of consciousness (though the likeness has only recently been acknowledged) is not fundamentally different from that proposed by William James in the 1890s, when he said that "a man has as many social selves as there are individuals who recognize him." James believed that it is futile to try to distinguish the "subjective life . . . from the objects known by its means," that—as we would later learn to say—the self is authored by the world rather than the other way around. What this amounts to is the conclusion that it is unintelligible to talk about the self before the advent of language. Language reveals itself as the medium in which the endless relationships that we call consciousness have their birth and in which they spend their life.

Once one arrives at such a view of the sovereignty of language, there are two directions, I think, in which it is possible to proceed. One is to go the way of Emerson, to savor and celebrate the infinite proliferation of perceptions and expressions (two terms for the same thing) that constitute the always-growing self. The other is to denounce the entanglement of the self in language and to seek some escape from the web. It is this second response that has emerged as the overwhelming and, I believe, misguided choice of our profession, and that accounts for the growing irrelevance of the academic critic for people who like to read.

Why it happened this way is a complex historical question that all the polemics from both sides of what is conventionally called "the culture wars" have, in my opinion, barely broached. We seem beset by a longing to rid the world of moral ambiguity and hypocrisy, which is our word for certain kinds of inconsistencies between word, motive, and act. The trouble is that to fulfill this longing for a prelinguistic ideal, one must be willing to sacrifice irony and wit, which involve the joyful manipulation of words (this is why the word "wicked," for example, may be used to describe a bad character as well as a good joke). In such a purified world, there is no room for literature.

Those who seek such a world ask their students to take a kind of loyalty oath to gain membership in a self-proclaimed community of the pure—to live, that is, without the corrupting linguistic structures in which everyone else is still enveloped. They repudiate the ways we used to organize the world along demarcation lines between, say, East and West, Male and Female, Good and Evil, and they demand that we give up the geography these terms once gave us. They scout old metaphors and decry them (as I discovered when I once used the word "emasculated" in a public talk to describe a weak prose style and nearly caused a feminist riot). And they brook no opposition.

While the purge goes on—and despite some signs of increased resistance it does go on—a few critical voices have been raised on behalf of the other kind of response. This is the aesthetic response to our discovery that language invades us, indeed *is* us. Recently, the critic Frank Lentricchia has repudiated the party of theory to which he once belonged. "Tell me your theory," he writes, "and I'll tell you in advance what you'll say about any work of literature, especially those you haven't read." Other estimable critics have raised their voices against a profession that no longer does very well at introducing students to the "experience of intense delight" (Barbara Packer's phrase) that has always been the best reason to undertake literary study in the first place.

Among the dissenting critics, one of the least discourageable is Richard Poirier, who has been in the wars a long time. Poirier puts well the aesthetic truth worth fighting for:

> A literary text, any text, generates itself, word by word, only by compliance with or resistance to forms of language already available to it. The impulse to resist, or at least to modify, is necessarily stronger than is the impulse to comply, but the two factors coexist in a sort of pleasurable agitation which often evokes the image of sexual intercourse.

The idea of language upon which this statement is based is not fundamentally incompatible with the view—whether one calls it postmodernist or pragmatist—that language has an immense power to shape and constrain us. The difference is that those who read in Poirier's spirit are willing prisoners. They regard language as what Melville called (speaking of his stay among the Polynesians) an "indulgent captivity."

This book is about writers who make me grateful to have been captured. These writers believed, with William James, that "our descriptions" of the world are "themselves important additions to reality" and that "the great question" about how we describe the world is: "Does it, with our additions, rise or fall in value?" I celebrate them because I have no doubt that the world is better for their having written, and because I believe it is the responsibility of the critic to incite others to read them.

Acknowledgments

Much of this book appeared in earlier form under the editorship of several remarkable people to whom I owe more than dutiful thanks. A dozen years ago, Leon Wieseltier gave me the opportunity to write for an audience beyond the academy, and ever since, he has allowed me space and range while never settling for less than the best prose of which I am capable. For most of those years, his superb colleague at *The New Republic* Ann Hulbert held me to her own exacting standards. This book is stronger for their attention and concern, and some of it would never have been written without them. I am also grateful to Richard Poirier, Barbara Epstein, and Robert Boyers, all of them demanding readers of great integrity. As the book took form from these beginnings, Elisabeth Sifton helped me in innumerable ways to bring it to fruition. Virginia Barber not only represented but improved it. And as always, my wife, Dawn, shared with me every stage of reflection and composition. I thank her for being my sharpest yet most tolerant critic.

Index

C

T

U

V

W